PRAISE FOR HUSTON SMITH
AND HIS PREVIOUS BOOKS

"My idea of heaven (on earth) is sitting in a room and listening to Huston Smith."

— Pico Iyer, author of *The Global Soul*

"Sometimes [Huston Smith] becomes as spontaneous and radiant as the ineffable beauty he talks about.....A clean wind of truth blows through his presence. He always makes me feel more alive! He knows, and lives, and loves whereof he speaks."

— Coleman Barks, author of *Rumi: The Big Red Book*

"I read Huston Smith's *The World's Religions* as a teenager. It was the most influential event in my life. He has shaped my thinking and my lifelong quest, and guided me to where I am today."

— Deepak Chopra, author of
The Seven Spiritual Laws of Success and *War of the Worldviews*

"Huston Smith's words serve me well in traversing my spiritual path."

— Ram Dass, author of *Be Here Now*

"Huston Smith approaches religion with the wisdom of a philosopher and the wonder of a child. He looks for similarities that unite, not differences that divide. He comes armed with knowledge and blessed with understanding."

— Don Lattin, author of *The Harvard Psychedelic Club*

"[*The World's Religions*] is the one book on religion I can't do without. I return to it often — and always with reward."

— Bill Moyers

And Live Rejoicing

To Mary Jean,
to joy!

OTHER BOOKS BY HUSTON SMITH

The Almost Chosen People (with Kendra Smith)

Beyond the Post-Modern Mind

Buddhism: A Concise Introduction (with Phil Novak)

Cleansing the Doors of Perception: The Religious Significance of Entheogenic Plants and Chemicals

Condemned to Meaning

Forgotten Truth: The Common Vision of the World's Religions

The Huston Smith Reader (with Jeffery Paine)

Primordial Truth and Postmodern Theology (with David Ray Griffin)

The Purposes of Higher Education

The Religions of Man

The Search for America (editor)

A Seat at the Table: In Conversation with Native Americans on Religious Freedom (with Phil Cousineau)

The Soul of Christianity: Restoring the Great Tradition

Tales of Wonder: Adventures Chasing the Divine (with Jeffery Paine)

The Way Things Are: Conversations with Huston Smith on the Spiritual Life (with Phil Cousineau)

Why Religion Matters: The Fate of the Human Spirit in an Age of Disbelief

The World's Religions (revised and expanded edition of *The Religions of Man*)

And Live Rejoicing

Chapters from a Charmed Life

Personal Encounters with Spiritual Mavericks, Remarkable Seekers, and the World's Great Religious Leaders

HUSTON SMITH
WITH PHIL COUSINEAU

New World Library
Novato, California

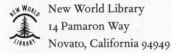

New World Library
14 Pamaron Way
Novato, California 94949

Text design by Tona Pearce Myers

Library of Congress Cataloging-in-Publication Data
Smith, Huston.
 And live rejoicing : chapters from a charmed life : personal encounters with spiritual mavericks, remarkable seekers, and the world's great religious leaders / Huston Smith with Phil Cousineau.
    p.   cm.
Includes bibliographical references (p. 195) and index.
ISBN 978-1-60868-071-9 (pbk. : alk. paper)
1. Smith, Huston. 2. Religion historians—United States—Biography. 3. Religions. 4. Religious leaders. I. Cousineau, Phil. II. Title.
BL43.S64A3 2012
200.92—dc23
[B]   2012016876

First printing, September 2012
ISBN 978-1-60868-071-9
Printed in the USA on 100% postconsumer-waste recycled paper

New World Library is proud to be a Gold Certified Environmentally Responsible Publisher. Publisher certification awarded by Green Press Initiative. www.greenpressinitiative.org

10 9 8 7 6 5 4 3 2 1

To our grandchildren,
Serena, Sierra, Isaiah, and Antonio,

and to our great-grandchildren,
Aubrey, Gil, and Sasha

First, a shudder runs through me,
and then the old awe steals over me.

— adapted from Plato's *Phaedrus*

Contents

Prologue

Oh, Happy Day

My earlier autobiographical *Tales of Wonder* sketched the outline of my life and those moments that helped illuminate my path. This sequel fills it in by describing episodes — way stations or stepping-stones, if you will — that stand out as exceptionally significant in connecting to the title of this volume. These episodes and encounters reveal many of the influences in my life that have affirmed a life of joy, even in this vale of sorrow.

Many readers will recognize that I have drawn the title of this book from "Oh, Happy Day! " a mid-eighteenth-century hymn by English clergyman Philip Doddridge (based on Acts 8:35), which was popularized by the gospel group the Edwin Hawkins Singers in 1967, and later by folksinger Joan Baez in 1971. The key stanza describes my outlook in life:

Oh happy day, oh happy day,
When Jesus washed my sins away.
He taught us how to watch and pray,
And live rejoicing every day;
Oh happy day, oh happy day,
When Jesus washed my sins away.

I gloss that hymn as follows: Happiness is the human birthright, and by extension we ought to cash in on that birthright and live rejoicing every day. We do this without denying — it must immediately be added — that sooner or later we all encounter tragedies that will beset us and show us that life is not a nonstop joyride. As the title of a true story (camouflaged as a best-selling novel) has it, *I Never Promised You a Rose Garden*.

Still, life's challenge is to make the joy an inclusive, all-embracing category that encompasses tragedy and transforms it in the way that Brother Lawrence of the Resurrection, a seventeenth-century Carmelite monk, articulated: "When we are persuaded that it is the hand of God that is acting in our lives, and that it is our Father, full of love, that allows us this state of humiliation, pain, and suffering, then all the bitterness is removed from them and they contain only sweetness."

That sweetness bodies forth in a second song from the nineteenth century, *My Life Flows On (How Can I Keep from Singing?)*, which was written in 1868 by the American minister Robert Lowry:

My life flows on in endless song,
Above earth's lamentation.
I hear the sweet, tho' far-off hymn
that hails a new creation.
Through all the tumult and the strife
I hear that music ringing;

It finds an echo in my soul —
How can I keep from singing?

Finally, who can forget the challenging words of the Roman poet Horace, who wrote something in the first century that has echoed down the centuries for two millennia: *Carpe diem*, or, "Seize the day." That phrase is bandied about, but few people are aware of the second half of the original expression: "Rejoice while you are alive."

Many seize the day, but how many seize it *rejoicingly*? I have tried to do both. Next I would like to mention four experiences, or stepping-stones, that set the direction for joyful living. As I look back over my life I can detect a pattern of series of experiences that either pointed me toward or reaffirmed my lasting conviction that we are in good hands, and in gratitude for that fact we should do everything we can to maximize our human potential for happiness.

THE FIRST STEPPING-STONE
TOWARD A LIFE OF REJOICING

In planning our family's first round-the-world trip I worked closely with my wife, Kendra, to arrange our travels. The Alhambra in Spain was high on the list of must-see places. Our friends had raved about it, saying that back in the eleventh century Moorish influence had created a new kind of architecture. However, I faced a deadline for submitting my book to Harper & Row Publishers, *The Religions of Man* (later retitled *The World's Religions*). I had hoped to mail it to the publisher before I left home, but I didn't make the deadline.

Once we were on the journey in Spain, I was usually too tired from long days of sightseeing to make much progress on the book in the evenings. By the time we arrived in Granada, where the

Alhambra has revealed its ancient beauty and wisdom for more than 650 years, I was consumed with guilt. I decided to bite the bullet and get back to work, even if it meant missing one of the great architectural masterpieces of the world.

Meanwhile, Kendra visited the magnificent Moorish palace, sometimes called "The Red Fortress," by herself while I worked on the manuscript. I was confident I would see the palace on another trip. That evening I took my supper in a nearby restaurant and then returned to our hotel room. Soon after there came a knock at the door. When I opened it there stood Kendra in all her glory. I was ecstatic to see her! She said that as a single woman traveling alone she been hassled on the palace grounds so much that she had decided to forgo the visit.

Needless to say, the moment I set eyes on her the idea of writing went out the door. We were so happy to be back together, we didn't even need to make love because the love in that room was so thick you could have cut it with a knife. I look back on that evening as a superlative moment of rejoicing.

THE SECOND STEPPING-STONE

When we were in Bombay, the area where we were staying was awash in colorful flyers announcing that a fully enlightened guru was in a town about thirty miles to the north. The flyer added that the guru would be giving *darshan*, a beautiful Sanskrit word describing the transfusion of spiritual energy that occurs when a fully realized master gazes directly into the eyes of a disciple.

Now, (as Dr. Richard Selzer wrote) I am not so leathery a skeptic as to willfully ignore an alert from the gods, so despite the fact that I was dubious and riddled with suspicions of bamboozlement, I picked up a flyer and boarded a bus that took me to the designated location. I arrived at nine o'clock in the morning, and though the temple was already packed with devotees, I managed to squeeze myself into a space on the floor.

Total silence.

After an hour or so someone appeared and said that the holy man — Swami Nityananda — would appear two hours later, around eleven o'clock. That hour came and passed. Around noon it was announced that the "manifestation" would occur at two o'clock.

With each announcement a number of devotees exited the temple, but I resolutely remained. Another four hours passed, and at six o'clock I was the only remaining supplicant.

Finally, after eight hours of waiting, the priest of the temple appeared, paused for a moment, and then beckoned me to follow him out the door at the rear of the sanctuary. There I saw a man in a dhoti squatting in the middle of the alley munching on a stick of sugarcane. He looked at me for a few intense moments, and I knew then and there I had received the object of my visit, my *darshan*.

Now, *darshans* vary widely. Some recipients swoon from them; others fall back as if someone had knocked them over. I have witnessed all these responses in others, but I am a low-key recipient. I continue to feel that if the master is real, *something* does happen. I played it safe by leaving after that brief gaze.

Exhilarated by my encounter, I dashed for the bus stop and managed to catch the last bus of the day back to Bombay. Upon arrival I found a taxi, which took me to our hotel, and I headed straight for the dining room, fearing that Kendra might have already eaten her supper or, worse, left the dining area.

Fortunately for me, she hadn't. She had patiently waited for me until a waiter told her that the dining room was about to close. She was still waiting when I walked in and she looked as happy to see me as I was to see her.

I had received my traditional dose of *darshan*, and now I was having another infusion of energy, another kind of gazing into a human being's eyes, but this time it was those of my own wife, over supper.

THE THIRD STEPPING-STONE

This third stepping-stone was very different.

Along with Kendra and our three daughters, I was living in St. Louis during the 1950s, where I was teaching at Washington University. In those days there was no air-conditioning, and the city was notorious for its stifling heat. Many people evacuated in the summer to escape the combination of heat and humidity that rose like steam from the confluence of the Mississippi and Missouri Rivers. One escaped if one possibly could. We did that by buying a cottage a day's drive away, on the southeastern shore of Lake Michigan, near a town called Ludington. It wasn't much of a cottage, very simple, but we were able to buy it. We became so fond of it we were inspired to name it Nikomis, a local Native American word meaning "eagle's nest."

Since it was such a long drive from St. Louis to that cottage we had to "break journey," as we used to say, along the way. We did this by spending the night with a cousin's family in Springfield, Illinois. On this particular summer evening, my cousin said they would be away but that they would leave the house key under the doormat. With old-world hospitality, they invited us to make ourselves at home.

Our evening was comfortable, and we rested from the long drive. Everything was proceeding as planned. But just before four in the morning I awoke with a sense of stinging exultation. I had the sudden and glorious realization that we hadn't simply escaped the sweltering heat of St. Louis and had a cool swim in Lake Michigan ahead of us that day. No, what hit me the hardest was knowing that I was about to enjoy two and a half months of uninterrupted freedom to write, and not just anything: I was suddenly free to write the book on world religions that had been hatching in my mind for many years and that would be my most widely read, reprinted, and translated book.

I was ecstatic at the prospect of having no professional duties, no phone calls to make, no letters to answer. I had my little Remington typewriter, a 160-degree panoramic view of the lake, and no responsibilities.

I was raring to go.

That's why I woke up so happy. Slowly, I shook Kendra until she woke up, and then I whispered to her, "We need to get an early start!" She smiled, and together we woke up our three dozing girls and piled into the car.

It was just before dawn when we headed north to the shores of Lake Michigan, and I felt an epiphany, some light in the darkness, a surge of rejoicing. I will never forget that sense of utter joy at the prospect of finishing the book that would define my life, the work I was destined to write.

THE FOURTH STEPPING-STONE

During the academic year 1944–1945, I spent the weeks writing my doctoral dissertation under a University of California professor in Berkeley. On the weekends I hitchhiked — which was easier then than it is now — seventy-five miles south to the weekend church near Monterey where I served because it had a cracker box–size parsonage attached to it. I needed a roof to put over the heads of Kendra and our toddler, Karen. So I gladly took the position.

When, on Friday evenings, I opened the parsonage door,

my daughter would greet me and go into the most fantastic foot-stomping dance imaginable. As soon as she finished her performance I would sweep her up into an embrace that soon included Kendra.

Although Karen was too young to speak, no words could have equaled that ecstatic dance she performed for me to express her love and her palpable joy at our reunions. Even the word *rejoicing* doesn't come close to doing justice to those weekend reunions. But it's close enough.

Acknowledgments

I would like to express my gratitude to Jon and Anna Monday, who spotted and corrected a number of serious errors in the early drafts of this book. Tenzin Kunsang was able to identify and correct a number of malfunctions in my word-processing machine. Gnpdup has maneuvered me through these recent years of declining physical strength, helping me do things I could not have done alone. I could not have hoped for a more competent and discerning editor for this book than Phil Cousineau has proved himself to be.

Georgia Hughes, editorial director of New World Library, contracted to publish this book and has been a model of patience in putting up with my innumerable overtakes and delays. Finally, John Loudon. He is now my agent who secured the contract for this book, but when he was an editor at HarperSanFrancisco (now HarperOne) he shepherded six of my books through to publication. What means the most to me, however, is that we have been friends for more than twenty years.

To all the above, I offer my sincerest thanks.

Introduction
by Phil Cousineau

At the center of religious life is a peculiar kind of joy,
the prospect of a happy ending that blossoms
from necessarily painful ordeals, the promise
of human difficulties embraced and overcome.

— HUSTON SMITH, *Yoga Journal*

In summer 2004 I met with Huston Smith at his home in Berkeley, California, to pore over the galleys of *The Way Things Are*, a scintillating collection of his interviews that I was editing at the time. Slowly, I realized, to my chagrin, that I had never asked him during our twenty years of friendship and collaborations if he had ever considered what W. Somerset Maugham called the "summing up." Perhaps I had refrained out of fear of sounding impertinent or, worse, naive, by asking that most callow, though essential, of questions, "What does it all *mean?*"

As I was deliberating over whether or not to pose the question, I came across a passage in the manuscript where Huston describes how the aim of his life's work had been to glean the "winnowed wisdom of the world."

So I decided to try to winnow Huston's wisdom.

"Huston," I said, "if someone had the temerity to ask you to compress what you've learned during your sixty or so years studying the great spiritual and philosophical systems, and then to condense those insights into some pithy advice for people who are searching for meaning in their lives, what would you say?"

The old professor pondered for a moment, an unusual response in this age of glib remarks, leaned back in his chair, and said, "I always know a good question when I hear one because I don't have a ready-made answer."

Then, he said quietly, "Follow the light, wherever it may lead."

Not only did I marvel at the poetry and beauty of his answer, but I was stunned by the synchronicity of the moment because I had encountered the same words only the day before.

"Huston, believe it or not, yesterday I was visiting Ansel Adams's family home in Carmel and discovered that he had once written on a simple index card a kind of motto for his life as a photographer: "Follow the light.""

Naturally, Huston was delighted.

While he had been following the inner light of the spiritual life, Adams had been following the outer light found in nature, their point of overlap being illumination itself. Wherever it may lead.

A LIFE OF REJOICING

This motto provides us with a luminous opening for *And Live Rejoicing*, the second volume of Huston Smith's memoirs. To complement the narrative style of his first volume, *Tales of Wonder*, this book is a mosaic of memories tied together by the single sublime theme hinted at in its title. From his exotic childhood growing up in rural China to his meetings with many of the most remarkable men and women of our time, Smith's life has been inspired by the unswerving conviction that we are "in good hands." And because of that dazzling gift, he has long believed that we should live with "infinite gratitude."

Huston's sense of joy at the sheer miracle of existence permeates these pages. Not only has working alongside him as the editor of the manuscript been fascinating in terms of learning about the extent of his ramblings around the globe and his fascinating friendships, but it has also helped resolve a mystery that has eluded me since our first in-depth conversation, on an airplane flying to Santa Fe to work with Gary Rhine on our documentary film, *The Peyote Road*.

How is it, I've wondered, that he has been able to maintain a sense of *equanimity*, that wonderful old-fashioned word for composure, despite the inevitable sorrows of life? So often I've watched him cast a spell over an audience, whether in our filmed interviews, public lectures, or book readings, all the while knowing of the personal tragedies he had endured or the existential pain he was feeling over the political upheavals and religious turbulence of our time.

How could he carry on? How was he able to leave his audiences spellbound? Was it by dint of sheer intellect? Or was it something more elusive? Could it be connected to the attitude he has cultivated that has allowed him to rejoice, regardless of circumstances?

THE ENIGMA OF ENIGMAS

After working on these memoirs this past year and combing through twenty years of notes from our conversations and interviews, I believe this collection of stories and reflections holds tantalizing clues to the enigma of the well-lived life. If it is true, as one of Huston's philosophical models, Socrates, said, "The unexamined life is not worth living," then it only stands to reason that the *deeply* examined life — and not only examined, but scoured for meaning — is *well* worth living.

What emerge in the following pages are exotic vignettes of Smith's spiritual upbringing as the child of missionary parents, which accounts for some of the impetus behind what he once told me was his "pilgrim's journey to truth." But far more is revealed here, such as his passion for writing, teaching, family life, and the cultivation of stimulating and challenging friendships with people from D. T. Suzuki to Saul Bellow, Thomas Merton to Vine Deloria Jr.

Despite enduring the grievous loss of a daughter to sarcoma, an especially vicious form of cancer, and a granddaughter to a tragic death aboard a boat in the South Pacific, the slings and arrows of criticism from the battlements of the academic world, and now — in his twilight years, afflicted with osteoporosis decompressing his spine — what he calls "the infirmities of old age," Huston has held on to his optimism and kept his balance. My sense is that he has been able to do so by focusing on what he describes as "what is truly worth knowing" by using a kind of binocular vision, with one eye focused on eternity, the other on the pressing social issues of the day. In this way, he has helped resolve those two images into one, affording himself, and us, a view of what he has deftly described as the "other world."

Not that he takes credit for this perspective or practice. He once confessed to me that he had always felt like a bit of an ancestor worshipper, perhaps a reflection of growing up in a world steeped in Confucian thought. "I'm not really an original thinker," he said, citing the much-revered Chinese philosopher, "but I am a lover of the ancients."

By deflecting credit, influence, and fame, Huston has cultivated the uncanny ability to let the wisdom of the ages shine *through* him rather than *on* him. Or, in the words of our mutual friend

Joseph Campbell, he has become "transparent to the transcendent." By steering the cultural attention to many of the world's religions and philosophical systems that have been ignored for too long, Smith's books and lectures have provided windows through which we may see the light and realize that we carry the light as well.

In this age of chest-thumping self-promotion, this is no easy task. His transparency, as expressed through crystalline prose and a clarion-clear public speaking style, has allowed two generations of readers and audiences to experience for themselves the poetic truths at the heart of the world's wisdom traditions. Moreover, he has demonstrated in his work and his daily life the spiritual imperative of love and compassion. The most moving example of this came when he sent me the following untitled poem by his daughter Karen, which he and his wife, Kendra, had found when they went through Karen's belongings after she died.

> Valentine's Day, that's when I knew;
> Doctor called, said, "Karen, you're through.
> Don't like bad news, goodness no,
> But those cancer bugs have gone through you and they'll
> Never let you go."
> So now's the time for tears that will never end:
> Knew life wasn't ready for mine to end.
> Say goodbye to my children, I always loved you so;
> Say goodbye to my grandchildren, the ones I'll never know;
> Say goodbye to my husband, as I lean my head on your chest:
> Good times, bad times, you were the best.

"I find it poignant," Huston wrote in the margins of the poem, "to the point that it still brings tears to my eyes."

When I read those words my mind moved slantwise to one of the most moving scenes in all of literature, which comes in Virgil's

Aeneid, when Aeneas watches Troy burn. "*Sunt lacrimae rerum et mentem mortalia tangunt*," wrote the visionary poet. "These are the tears of things, and our mortality cuts to the heart."

The capacity to feel the full spectrum of human emotion, from rapture to grief, and to convey those fully fathomed feelings to others is at the heart of all who strive to find the poetry, the truth, the soul of life. Perhaps that is why Huston once confided to me, after a lecture we gave at UCLA, that if he were to be reincarnated he would like to come back as a poet.

STAYING POSITIVE

One night, in 2004, we sat onstage together in dialogue for the prestigious Mind & Supermind lecture series in Santa Barbara. After a rousing ninety-minute exchange, we opened the question-and-answer session, in which Huston was asked, "How can you stay so positive in this vale of sorrow?"

"Well," Huston began slowly, "I don't *exactly* know; it hasn't been completely conscious. A single anecdote will suffice. On my last day at Central College, in Fayette, Missouri, my roommate told me something startling. 'Huston,' he said, 'Did you know that every morning for the past four years when you woke up your first word was always '*Good!*'?"

> *Do you know why angels can fly? Because they take themselves lightly.*
>
> — HUSTON SMITH, to Jack Cousineau, 2006

Naturally, the audience roared in approval but also in recognition of an unexpected insight into the art of living. That single, exultant syllable — *Good!* — combined Huston's youthful exuberance with the triumphant spirit of the Jewish mystics, who, he once told me, used to walk at the front of crowds with the Torah before them shouting, "Make way, make way for the image of the Lord!"

"But what should *we* make way *for*?" I later asked him.

"Well, the truth," he said. "What else would we be looking for?"

As an illustration of *esprit de l'escalier* (the spirit of the staircase), I wish I had answered "contribution" at the time, because that too has proved to be one of the sources of his indefatigable energy and productivity. To cite Martin Luther King Jr., whom Huston once hosted, "Life's most persistent and urgent question is: what are you doing for others?"

For Huston Smith, the answer would be writing and teaching. As he recently told me over lunch at his favorite Thai restaurant in Berkeley, "People always have a craving for the right orientation, and they come to my classes and read my books hoping to find that orientation."

THE SONG OF THE OPEN ROAD

In spring 2009 my great friend the songwriter, musician, and playwright R. B. Morris, of Knoxville, Tennessee, rode with me to Berkeley to pick up Huston for one of the many luscious Thai lunches we have shared over the years. When I told Huston that R. B. was a singer, he said, "Oh, singing is my favorite part of the day. Did you know that the times when we are singing are the only times that all the circuits of the brain light up?" Delighted to share that piece of science with us, Huston turned around and shouted into the backseat to make sure R. B. could hear him, "It's *healthy!*" stretching the two syllables into seven, like a revival preacher in a tent singing out *Hallelujah!*

> *Beware of the differences that blind us to the unity that binds us.*
> — HUSTON SMITH,
> *The Way Things Are*

"Did *you* know," R. B. asked him, playfully, "that Bob Dylan once said, 'I don't belong to any church, but when I *sing* the gospels, I *believe*! Singing songs like *A Closer Walk with Thee* and *Rock of Ages* makes me *believe*.'"

Huston's eyes lit up like a pinball machine.

"I rest my case!" he shouted, again, this time triumphantly. Then he asked, "So, do you want to sing a song?"

"Sure, Huston," said R. B. with a grin as wide as his guitar. "I'm game. How about 'Old Copper Penny?' " R. B. then sang his ballad a cappella while Huston listened as if he were in a church pew and not the front seat of a car. Moments after he finished, Huston asked, "Now can we sing one *together*?"

"What do you have in mind?"

"How about a Pete Seeger song?"

As we drove along Shattuck Avenue Huston sang like a troubadour, leading us in a rousing version of "If I Had a Hammer," by one of Huston's oldest friends, the legendary folksinger Pete Seeger.

Now, that's what I call rejoicing.

THE TRUE MEANING OF RELIGION

When I first heard Huston's story about teaching a group of East Bay schoolkids the essence of Zen, sitting quietly, doing nothing, if even for a few minutes, I invited him to give an informal talk to the students of Cathedral School for Boys, in San Francisco, where my son Jack, his honorary godson, was then in the fifth grade.

As the boys noisily shuffled into the choir behind the altar at Grace Cathedral, Huston's face grew pensive. I had been with him onstage numerous times but had never seen this side of him. He was as much in awe of them as they were of him.

While the boys looked down at their notes (for they had been prompted to bring questions for the famous visiting professor), Huston turned to me and shouted, "Oh, this is wonderful. Looking out at their faces is like...well, words escape me. But it's like looking out over a field of flowers. They are so fresh and colorful and innocent."

Rather than complain about being hauled across the bay at 8:30

in the morning to talk to a bunch of kids, he was *rejoicing* in the opportunity to discuss his favorite topic — religion — with them. When one brave fifth grader, Christian Bolles, asked him what was so special about religion, Huston said without hesitation, "It reminds that we are in *good hands*, and because of that we should be grateful." On the ride back to Berkeley, I asked him why he seemed so happy.

"It's simple," he said. "Everyone, including children, is looking for *orientation*, a direction, an anchor in life. I hope I gave that to them today."

For me, it is moments like these that reflect the numinous aspect of the word that has dominated Huston's life — *religion*, whose origins lie in the Latin *religare*, which means "bind together," and can mean both holding without letting go and holding together for solace and security.

> *It almost seems like it was masterminded for me to be in the right place at the right time.*
>
> — HUSTON SMITH,
> *San Francisco Chronicle,*
> May 21, 2009

REJOICE, REGARDLESS

To conclude, I would like to cite one more anecdote from the luminous lunch that my friend R. B. and I shared with Huston. After a marvelous, far-ranging discussion about music, travel, and books we had recently read, Huston became pensive.

"Lately," he said, "I have been reading that beautiful book by Norman Maclean, *A River Runs Through It*. Those last lines seem to express what I am feeling these days, as I near my ninth decade." And then Huston stunned us by reciting by heart the last paragraph of that wistfully beautiful and painful book: "I am an old man now.... Most of my friends have passed away.... All of my memories have shifted and faded. But there is one thing I remember... the rivers that run through my life. I am haunted by rivers."

At that moment I saw his life, and all our lives, as water, swiftly moving, inexorably passing us by, like time itself, and yet something to see beauty in, to rejoice in. That is the Huston Smith who emerges in this book, the one who once confided to me that his life had been no more than a "pilgrim's journey to find the truth."

I hope that you find in the stories that follow the inspiration and beauty that one of Huston's own favorite poets, the thirteenth-century Sufi mystic Jalaluddin Rumi, referred to when he wrote, "Whoever travels without a guide, needs two hundred years for a two-day journey." I trust you will find some guidance here from a trustworthy guide about how to forge your own well-lived and rejoicing life.

Part I

Chapter One

Saving the Moon and Other Memories of a Boyhood in China

G iven my age, I may be the only person still living who witnessed the moon being saved.

My parents were missionaries, and I grew up in a Chinese town, Dzang Zok, about seventy miles from Shanghai. One night, when I was about ten years old, we heard an alert that the moon was in danger, a deafening din that woke us in the middle of the night. We knew from this noise that the dragon — the Chinese symbol of terror, awe, and might — was swallowing the moon and had to be scared away. So the townsfolk seized whatever noisemakers they could lay their hands on, such as pots and pans, to bang with large wooden spoons, and put them to frantic use. The strategy of noisemaking always prevailed. When the eclipse was total, the dragon eventually disgorged its prey, and the moon was soon safely back in the sky.

When I think about that exciting night, I ponder the fact that there we were, an American family surrounded by our Chinese neighbors, alike in our human capacities but worlds apart in our outlooks.

Today, more then eight decades later, I muse on that wondrous opportunity to experience two such radically distinct worlds. One world was populated with fire-breathing dragons, and the other features the Hubble telescope and all the other stunning discoveries of modern astronomy. Let me tell you more about growing up in China.

MY FAMILY IN TRADITIONAL CHINA

I was born in 1919, the second-oldest son to my parents, Wesley and Alice Smith. Our mother was born in China, for her parents were also missionaries, which means that my family's missionary lineage dates back to the middle of the nineteenth century. We children were privy to a way of life that was relatively unchanged from the previous century and has since vanished into history.

My mother was fond of telling stories about the exotic side of China. I remember seeing a photograph of a man being carried in a sedan chair. Our mother told us that in the early days in China women were not to be seen outside their homes. To "go abroad," as we said in those days, meaning to leave the house, women had to be carried in sedan chairs that were completely encased in black cloth.

Occasionally, she would see on the streets of our town an elderly Chinese man with fingernails on one hand that were eight inches long. The arm was secured by some means to the opposite shoulder and moved so infrequently that it was virtually paralyzed. The point of this strange practice of growing such long fingernails was to underscore the fact that the man was a scholar, a much-revered profession in old China, and did not have to work for a living.

Around the same time, 1929 or 1930, with America mired in the Depression, my parents showed us a photograph that our grandparents had taken of a man who had been caught stealing. In China's marginal economy, prisons were out of the question, so the Chinese devised an ingenious alternative that local authorities meted out as punishment, the *cangue*, which dated back to at least the Ming dynasty. The invention was something like the pillory in the West, but portable. It was a square board with sides slightly longer than the length of the upper arm, and it was cut in half, with a half-circle in each half, so that when the boards were joined they would encircle a thief's neck. Fasten the boards together and — voilà! — you had a mobile prison. The prisoner could neither feed himself nor lie down without the help of his "jailers." What was perhaps even worse was the fact that the erstwhile thief was wandering the streets, unable to go home, and was being publicly shamed, which meant he lost face, almost the worst of fates in traditional China.

The punishment was so effective and inexpensive that one wonders why it was given up. I suspect it was because the Chinese didn't like to air their dirty laundry in public.

Traditional China was a meritocracy, and it produced another peculiar practice witnessed by our family. Every three years, government examinations were given in different parts of the country. One of those sites was in Nanking (the Chinese pronunciation is "Nanjing"), and its examination hall was close to the house where our mother had spent several years of her childhood. The hall was divided into cubicles large enough to contain only a bed, a table, a chair, and a commode.

The examination consisted of a single question — and it was the same question year after year — namely, to write about the Confucian classics. For the theory was that the study of those classics taught students to think for themselves. The classics were considered so important that government positions were given each year to the students with the highest scores. To prevent cheating, students were locked into those cubicles for the two days allotted for the examination. Food and water were pushed through an open slot at the bottom of the door.

One day, when she was a little girl, my mother was shown a *pony*, a crib sheet that a student had used on an examination. Knowing that the exam would determine whether or not he would receive a government position, the cheating student had written the classics in tiny characters on the lining of his gown and copied them onto the page provided by the school. The competition among the thousands who took the examinations was fierce; the students lived under a terrible strain. When it was all over, a student was occasionally found to have lost his mind, actually gone mad from the stress. The cheat sheet was social history. Today it would be hung in a museum.

The basic concept of studying the classics still strikes me as sound — not the emphasis on rote memory, but this type of meritocracy. What would our nation be like if it were ruled by intelligence instead of the hugely bankrolled campaigning that currently tips our own elections?

A WORLD OF NEVER AGAINS

With that brief dip into my mother's China, I will return to my own childhood there. The world that I grew up in, rural China near Shanghai in the 1920s, was a world, as I stated in *Tales of Wonder*, my first volume of memoirs, of *never agains*.

Never again will there be a city of a hundred thousand inhabitants that has never known an engine, a machine, or even a bicycle and has no telephones or electricity, though our family had a small coal-stoked generator that produced enough electricity to light our house.

Never again will there be a city of such size where the only outdoor sound that can be heard after dark is the barking of stray dogs. Hoping to quiet them, we first threw rocks at them from an upstairs window but soon discovered that pieces of coal worked even better because they shattered.

Never again will there be a place where the single-page newspaper is pasted to the walls in various parts of the city so it can be read by the 20 percent of the population that is literate.

Never again will there be a place where there is no pollution and stars hang so close overhead that one can imagine one is viewing them from the Himalayan peaks.

Never again will there be a place where men pull passengers in two-wheeled carriages known as rickshaws or carry them in sedan chairs, on which two men with flat poles on their shoulders carry passengers.

Never again will we have towns where the most conspicuous religion is folk religion and where bottles are positioned horizontally over the lintels of doors with their noses pointed outward to simulate cannons — it was believed they could warn evil spirits and that if these spirits tried to enter town they would be blown to smithereens.

Never again will there be a place where one can be awakened in the middle of the night by the piercing stench of night soil that is being carried to fertilize rice paddies.

Never again will the world hear the cry *ting wou* — "bowls mended" — by an itinerant craftsman who is vending his skill. I say never again because bowls today are made of plastic, which does not admit of clean breaks, and also because now it would be cheaper to simply replace a broken bowl than to mend it — even if we knew how to do that.

The list could be extended indefinitely, but I think that this is enough to make my point, and I hope I have given you a stronger sense of what my "never again" childhood was like.

RITUALS I REMEMBER

One of the other predominant memories I have from those early years in China is how crowded our hometown was. The houses shared common walls that divided their living quarters, and the town's labyrinthine lanes were so narrow that when I stretched out my arms, my hands touched the wooden walls of the houses on both sides of the lanes.

Even so, our back gate looked out over a vacant lot. The empty lot was reserved for the well-to-do in town, who had paper "death houses" built on them when they died. These death houses contained facsimiles of furniture, and often we would find genuine silk coverlets on the mock beds. The town's leading people streamed through the death houses to stare at the family's opulence and to revel in how the affluent lived.

At the appointed time of the funerals, Buddhist priests in their robes circumnavigated the death houses in a clockwise direction, chanting and playing their flutes. The sheaves of straw that were leaning on all sides of the house were ignited. The Buddhist priests circled the house as the house was engulfed in flames, carrying its ashen contents upward to serve the deceased in his afterlife.

On the last such occasion that I witnessed, a cardboard "death car" was parked by the front door of one of the cardboard death houses. It was surely one of the oddest sights of my life.

In the last such ceremony I attended, I witnessed the appearance of professional mourners, those who were hired by someone in the upper class to sit in at funerals from dawn till dusk. They were paid to weep and wail and pour out their souls.

Looking back on this memory it seems to me a perfect illustration of the sociologist Thorstein Veblen's influential theory of "conspicuous consumption," but on the other side of the world. The Chinese version of this social phenomenon was that only the rich could afford to hire mourners, called *chi ku* (in Wade-Giles transcription), which literally means a "bitterness-eater," those who were hired to devour the sorrow of those grieving at funerals.

A DEPRIVED OR A GIFTED CHILDHOOD?

Over the years some well-meaning people have suggested to me that it must have been hard to put up with the privations of my childhood growing up in rural China. But those people are wrong — dead wrong. For one thing, it never occurred to us children to think of being deprived, for we had never possessed, or even known about, many of the things that are commonplace today. Even now, as an adult in my twilight years, I don't think of myself as having been deprived, for growing up in China immeasurably enriched my life by expanding my experience. For I know about — and have *lived* — two different lives. Being raised in an ancient world meant owning far less paraphernalia, while my life in modern America has meant accumulating more encumbrances than I think are needed. I feel blessed by the good fortune that has come from living in two worlds in one lifetime.

CHINA'S WARLORDS

My family lived during a time when China's central government was weak and warlords battled one another for power and control. Twice in my childhood the American consulate in Shanghai sent word that for safety's sake we must leave our town the next morning and go to Shanghai. We were told in no uncertain terms we could only take with us what we could carry in our own two hands. Only on the second of these sudden evacuations was I old enough to understand what was really happening. Our parents told my brother Walter and I that we could each carry *one toy* on our escape. I took my beloved Peter Rabbit stuffed animal.

The next morning I watched as our father handed over the house key to Tsai Kung, our cook, not knowing if we would ever see him or our house again. I saw a single tear drop from Tsai Kung's eye onto the key, and we departed.

After four months the political situation settled down enough for us to return home and pick up where we had left off with our lives.

GUARDIAN ANGELS

During our sixty-seven years of marriage, my wife, Kendra, has often remarked that I seem to have a guardian angel perched on my left shoulder. On occasions I have had reason to think she was right.

My earliest memory is of being desperately thirsty as a young child when our area in China was suffering from a drought. One day when I was sick with flu my thirst was intensified by an interminable half-hour wait until I could have a teaspoon of cool water, because that was all that I could keep down without vomiting. But against heavy odds, I survived. All I could do then was endure the experience, but if I had had words to communicate thoughts, they would have expressed my gratitude and rejoicing that my life had been saved and that a future awaited me.

The future was far from assured, however. Twice again in my early years my life was almost snatched from me.

Dzang Zok, the city where we lived in China, abutted a hill, which as children we called a mountain because it was the highest we had ever seen. Our city was surrounded by a wall about thirty feet high. At 10:00 p.m. the gates in the city walls were closed and padlocked to prevent the looting of warlords and bandits, as discussed above.

One pleasant summer afternoon I decided to take a walk. I exited the North Gate and began to circumambulate the city wall counterclockwise. Incidentally, ours was one of three city walls in all of China that was round. All the others in the country were square. No one knows why there were these three exceptions.

When I had walked around the wall for about half a mile it occurred to me that I might climb over the wall and then almost roll down the hill to our house, which was at the bottom of it.

Let me insert a bit of contextual history here.

If it had been two centuries earlier, I could have walked a little farther around the city walls and entered the West Gate, but it had been walled up because a plague had decimated the city's inhabitants and the feng shui adepts said that the plague was being caused by evil spirits that were pouring through the West Gate. So, they declared, it had to be walled up. They also advised that a stubby pagoda be built on top of the hill to incarcerate any evil spirits that might escape.

I pondered my situation. The wall sloped inward as it ascended, and I noticed that it was tiered at each level and that the ledges could accommodate little more than half the width of a shoe if the shoe was placed sideways on them.

Glancing upward, I also noticed that the wall was thickly matted with heavy vines that I thought I could chin myself up on. The venture seemed feasible, so I started my climb.

As I ascended, however, the scene began to change in some worrisome ways. For one thing, the ledges were beginning to narrow to the point that they could no longer securely accommodate my feet. Also, the vines, having less soil to nurture them, were becoming sparser, and with less dirt for their roots to grip, they gave way at the slightest tug.

I became apprehensive. As I continued my climb, apprehension turned into panic. For what could I do? I couldn't descend, for

I couldn't see where to place my feet. As for ascending, the danger increased with every step, for the vines were coming out with the slightest tug.

Still, I had to do something, for I was growing more and more fatigued. So with no time to think, I slinked my body up to the wall and, hoping against hope that the precariously narrow grip of my left shoe would hold, I lunged upward and managed to get a left-handed, two-finger grip on the top of the wall, followed by a right-handed, four-finger grip. I chinned my body to the top of the wall, flopped over, and rolled down the hill to our house, exhausted but safe. Thank you, guardian angel.

SHANGHAI HIGH SCHOOL

I loved our town and its people. I can't imagine a place where I would rather have been raised, or that would have served as a better launching pad into my adult life. However, eventually I was ready to move from my mother's tutelage around the dining room table to the Shanghai American School, or SAS.

My transition from Dzang Zok to Shanghai was typical for children of missionaries. We were taught at home until eighth grade, then we went to Shanghai for high school, and then we were off to America. There was no real conversation about it. It was just expected.

I was excited to fly the coop.

The day before I left for high school, a journey that took five hours by launch to Soochow, or Zhugjo, in Mandarin, then three hours by train from there to Shanghai, my father took the opportunity to tell me, "We're sorry to see you go away to Shanghai, but we would be even sorrier to see you stay." They knew how good it would be for me to go.

My father also took the opportunity to cut my hair, to save having to pay a barber a quarter to do it. I pleaded with him not to shear me as short as he had shorn my brother when he left home for high school. For when my brother arrived at SAS his classmates said he looked like a convict, and this earned him the nickname of the infamous maximum security penitentiary, "Sing-Sing," which stuck with him for all four high school years.

Later, my mother told me that when she turned me over to the principal at SAS, her last words to him were, "Don't give up on Huston. He can get it. It just takes him longer."

She had discovered as she tutored me that I was a slow learner, for I am the middle of three sons, and both of the others learned quicker than I did. Even my younger brother was ahead of me in grammar. (I'm not even sure I know grammar today, but I believe I have developed an ear for the music of words. Who needs the rules, anyway?)

That the quality of a mind does not depend on its speed is a truth that has stood me in good stead as a teacher, for when a student stammered out a clumsy answer to a question, I gave her time to turn it over in her mind and then restate it in her own words. The reformulated answer was usually much better than the original one, and the student was pleased with what she had accomplished.

I had looked forward to the Shanghai American School, but I did not receive a warm welcome upon arrival. It was winter, and the window of the room to which I was assigned was open and the room was freezing cold. It turned out that my roommate, whom I had yet to meet, kept pigeons and left the window open so they could peck at the birdseed that he had sprinkled on the sill. The windowsill was covered with bird shit, but thank God the pigeons didn't enter the room.

For obvious reasons, my roommate was hanging out with his friends in their warm rooms. But I had yet to make any friends, so I spent that first afternoon in bed in my freezing room, clothed and with the covers pulled tightly over my shoulders. The ordeal was short-lived. After supper when it was dark, my roommate came back to our room and closed the window, and soon the radiator began to clank and warm the room. By then the pigeons had also retired to their nests.

One of the main reasons I learned to love SAS was that after being tutored by my mother around the dining room table since I was a child, studying with other students was exciting. I wasn't learning just from her anymore. Suddenly I had classmates, to say nothing of oodles of afterschool friends.

As proof of my mother's insight into my character, I dropped biology in my second year of high school and still vividly recall what happened the following year. When I reread the green textbook we had used for the class, I thought to myself, "Hey, this is intelligible now! The words make sense!" This was the last evidence of my being a slow learner. I was astonished to see how much things had changed from one year to the next.

School days were exciting, but then came the weekends. They were lonely. Most of the students were Shanghai residents and would go to their homes on weekends. For the first three weeks after Saturday lunch I would go to a playing field, stretch out on my stomach, bury my head on my forearms, and cry my heart out. My parents were back in my hometown, and so were the servants' children, who were my playmates and had been my only friends, and I wasn't with them. I missed them. I believed then that Dzang Zok was the only place I needed to grow up. My only friends were all back home. I was glad to have new friends, but I missed my family and my old friends terribly. That sadness lasted for three weekends, and then it was over. Those painful weekends taught me what it is like to be homesick.

ANOTHER ENCOUNTER WITH MY GUARDIAN ANGEL

While I was studying at the SAS my guardian angel saved my life once again. Our campus was in a walled compound that included classrooms, dormitories, and playing fields. There were always bi-cycles lying around, and one Saturday afternoon a friend and I decided to go for a ride.

Our school was located at the west edge of the city, so we headed out on a towpath that ran along the canal. I was in the lead, and very soon the path made a sharp turn to the right and plunged at a 45-degree angle toward two six-inch-wide boards that bridged the canal. The pitch was too steep for the cycle's brakes to hold, and anyway, if they had held I would have pitched headlong over the handlebars into the stagnant canal and breathed in and swal-lowed all manner of deadly germs. Considering the diseases that were ravaging Dzang Zok at that time, I very likely would have died of cholera.

I steered toward one of the six-inch planks, frantically trying to retain my balance without turning the bike wheels, and flopped to the ground safely on the other side of the canal.

Thanks again, angel.

Memory fails me as to how I and my bike got back to my friend, who, forewarned by my disaster, had managed to flop from his bike while there was still time. But my heart fills with joy to think I have had a guardian angel looking over my shoulder all these years.

HOLIDAYS

Three days of Thanksgiving vacation were not enough time to go home, but it was bearable because Christmas vacation was in sight. I looked forward immensely to returning home, but the journey was an ordeal. The three-hour train ride wasn't so bad, for at least my brother and I were out of the wind. But the five hours on the launch ride were an unmitigated torture. We had to keep wiggling our toes and our thinly gloved fingers to try to keep our circulation going. But we weren't too downcast because we knew our cook was going to be on the dock to meet us and guide us to our house. So we could keep going. He would guide my older brother and me in the year that we overlapped at SAS, but even when we arrived the ordeal wasn't over. When we got home, we were ordered to plunge our bare feet into a pail of near-freezing water in the hope of staving off chilblains. Still, we were happy. A warm supper awaited us, after which we would tumble into our warm beds, spent but infinitely happy.

DRAGON WELL

I was about to close this section on my early childhood in China when I remembered — the *well*.

When our family moved for a trial stint to our town, we lived in rented quarters, but when my parents were persuaded that Dzang Zok would be our family's permanent mission field, my father took things in hand. He located an empty plot of land, large enough for our family house and a smaller house for our servants' family. Then he set to work as both architect and contractor in having the two houses built with a thirty-foot-high encompassing wall that turned the interior into a compound.

My father also knew we would need water. Family friends had told him that they knew of a feng shui water wizard who could tell us where we would find underground water for the well he knew we needed to dig.

My headstrong father couldn't abide such nonsense. However, he measured a spot midway between our servants' quarters and our house, marked the spot, and then tried to hire local workmen to dig the well. What he had forgotten was that everything about us foreigners was food for gossip. The workers he tried to hire as diggers, having heard that the feng shui water wizards had not been consulted, told my father that the random digging was pointless. They told him that they didn't want him to waste his money.

Still, headstrong as he was, my father donned his work clothes and started digging anyway. Our neighbors gathered around to watch the drama unfold over the next several days.

First day's digging, no water.

Second day, no water.

So it went for six days.

On the seventh day my father didn't rest; he just kept digging, trying to conclude his efforts. That was when he noticed that as he dug deeper the dirt began to seem slightly damp. He tamped down the soil, climbed out of the hole, and with great resignation that he hadn't actually struck water yet, headed back to the house for supper.

Early the next morning, when he surveyed the area where he had been digging for a week he discovered to his astonishment that the hole was flooded to the brim with water.

The sight terrified the bystanders.

"You have scratched the back of the dragon," one of the local elders told my father. They were so scared they refused to help him even bail out the water so he could brick up the hole.

Thwarted, he bucketed out the water himself, then with great determination climbed back down into the hole and bricked up the bottom and the walls.

We had our well.

THE GREAT GOING FORTH

Eventually, there came the time for the Great Going Forth. Buddhists use that phrase for the night that Siddhartha Gautama turned away from his family and inheritance and set forth on the journey that would lead him to enlightenment and Buddhahood. For missionary children, though, it meant turning our backs on the China where we were born and raised and venturing across the Pacific Ocean to America, our native land, where we would spend the rest of our lives, punctuated here and there by travels abroad.

When it came time for me to go to America for college at age seventeen, one of my aunts (my father's sister, who was a missionary in Korea) offered to subsidize my return to America via the Trans-Siberian Railway — but only if I would wait a year until her furlough was due.

"No way!" I told my family. I was too eager to get to the fabled land of promise and get on with my life.

Eighteen days on the Pacific, with overnight stops in Nagasaki, Yokohama, and Honolulu, was an exciting prospect — I could hardly wait to leave.

Shipboard romance has now become a familiar phrase. In my youth I had never heard of it, but I can testify to its validity. I can still remember her name, Hilda Benson, and the college she was headed for, Gustavus Adolphus College, in Minnesota. The romance wasn't physical — we were too shy even to hold hands, and kissing didn't even enter our minds. Shuffleboard and Ping-Pong were about as far as it went. But it was, for sure, a real — and reciprocal — romance.

Many decades later, I was invited to lecture at that same Gustavus Adolphus College. I was surprised to find that Hilda's name was still recognized. She had become a member of the Board of Regents. I must admit that I was disappointed that she didn't come to my lecture. Perhaps she had died.

But I digress.

I have conflicting feelings about plane flights. On the one hand, flights have enabled me to visit places I would never have seen without them, and I am grateful to the airlines for that gift. On the other hand, I believe that the airlines have all but wiped out sea travel, except for luxury-liner holiday cruises in the

Caribbean, which is an entirely different story. So I lament the decline of ocean liners, partly because as part of a missionary family that enjoyed furloughs every year, we sailed from Shanghai to America by steamship many times.

I do not remember my first transpacific voyage, taken when I was six years old, but I vividly recall another voyage we took eight years later, when I was fourteen. My father arranged for us to visit the ship's engine room, which I found fascinating. I also remember playing shuffleboard and Ping-Pong on the swaying deck, and the flying fish that flashed with phosphorus when darkness fell.

At Honolulu we broke journey, which was always a highlight of the transpacific voyage. We were able to linger there in port for a day and a half, and one of our stops stands out, a visit to a local public garden where the night-blooming cereus were in full flower and the air smelled like perfume.

The departure pageants, though, were the most memorable aspects of our stay. Ship stewards paced the deck with trays filled with brightly colored streamers that passengers threw to those lining the dock to see us off. As the loops of rope that anchored the ship to the wharf were cast off from their gunwales the ship floated away. One by one the streamers broke free until only one remained. When it too snapped a cheer went up as if everyone were applauding its endurance and the beauty of its ritual.

The ship's band then launched into the poignant Hawaiian song "Aloha-oe," which begins, "Proudly sweeps the rainbow across the sky" and then proceeds to the refrain that was sung by those left on the dock and those leaving aboard the ship:

Farewell to thee, farewell to thee,
The winds will carry back my sad refrain.
One fond embrace, before we say good-bye
Until we meet again.

These memories washed over me during my two days in Honolulu. But something was different this time around. When I took the first sea voyage I knew we would be returning to China as a family. This time, at age seventeen, I was going to America alone, and for good. And in a wonderful way, I was also going home again.

Chapter Two

College Life in the Heartland

H istory and religion are the warp and woof of my life story. They often weave together so tightly that it is difficult to separate them.

During my parents' furloughs from being missionaries in China, our family spent its summers on the family farm in Missouri, where my father grew up. So I spent my adolescent summers, between 1923 and 1925, as well as two of my college summer vacations, down on the family farm.

For one week in July every evening was spent at a revival meeting in a nearby chapel. When I was six years old I helped round up the farm's two horses, Bell and Trot, and hitched them to the old buggy, which carried us five miles over gravel roads to the neighborhood chapel. When I returned years later for the first of my college summer vacations, my aunts, who ran the farm, had up-graded from the horse and buggy to a Ford Model T that I was able to ride in for the short trip to the revival meetings. The following summer they upgraded again, this time to a spiffy new Model A.

EVANGELICAL MEETINGS IN HISTORICAL PERSPECTIVE

Most of the immigrants that poured into America from England were followers of John Wesley, and those who adhered to his message were called "Methodists" because of the heavy emphasis that Wesley placed on the *method* of religious life he advocated. The message that Wesley brought to America was that the Church of England's reliance on the sacraments for salvation induced complacency. Wesley taught that what was needed was a personal resolve to forgo sinning and an adherence to that resolution. In short, he taught that a *conversion* to a radically different way of life was required.

The spiritual gatherings that were organized to keep Wesley's method securely on track were called revival meetings. In the eighteenth century their numbers, force, and momentum created historical surges that came to be called "awakenings." One of Wesley's followers, Jonathan Edwards (1703–1758), almost single-handedly launched America's First Great Awakening, in the eighteenth century. The Second Awakening occurred in the early nineteenth century, and my family entered the picture around the middle of that century.

Heartland America in my father's day was solidly Methodist. My father was actually christened Wesley Smith. By the time he was born, the fervor of the Second Awakening had declined, but it had left in its wake the hugely popular ritual of revival meetings. Whenever my father heard of a revival meeting within driving distance, he would load his wagon with provisions, such as food, blankets, and Bibles, and take off, leaving care of the farm to his sisters.

Typically, when he arrived at the meeting he would encounter many other wagons stationed in a large circle within which people congregated and socialized. The scene must have been reminiscent of the settling of the West, with folks exchanging stories and information at the great crossroads. Over the course of a revival meeting preachers sermonized, of course, but socializing was the main agenda. It must be remembered that in those days farming was a rather lonely occupation.

"Did you ever hear of sweet Bet, of Pike?" someone might ask a stranger. "She crossed the wide prairie with her husband Ike."

When I think of those grand gatherings another comparison comes to mind, the "be-ins," in San Francisco's famous Summer of Love, in 1967.

On a small scale, revival meetings dotted the heartland of America. July was the favorite and targeted month for these meetings. With the corn "knee high by the Fourth of July," as the song in *Oklahoma* goes, and threshing bees (when crews of men and boys would thresh the grain, and groups of women and girls would keep the threshing crew fed) at harvesttime comfortably in the future, July was the time reserved especially for religion, and in that spirit itinerant evangelist preachers roamed the land like circuit rodeo riders.

How vividly I remember being caught up in the excitement. These were dress-up occasions. Women wore their Sunday best, and even though Missouri can be hot and humid in July, jackets were required of men. However, on hot evenings it was acceptable to carry your pressed jacket, if it was neatly folded, over your arm.

I can still recall a mixture of thrill and dread as we approached the chapel, anticipation mounting, for we were on our way to meet

God. Believe me, dear reader, July in the heartland of America in the 1930s was all about religion.

The meetings themselves can easily be summarized. The chapel was invariably packed. Hymnbooks were in their racks, but they were seldom needed, for we knew our favorite hymns by heart. Three or four hymns would warm us up, and then the evangelist would ascend the two steps to the podium. His messages followed a standard format. They weren't your standard altar-call harangues, but neither were they typical sermons, as we understand the word today. Instead, these messages were heavily evangelistic. That meant they emphasized personal conversion and the inerrancy of the Bible, and they exhorted those of us at the revival meeting to stop misbehaving, or the consequences of our actions would catch up with us. The evangelists took every opportunity to deliver their never-out-of-place reminder to us that we should lead the righteous life.

The wrap-ups of the meetings were always brief. The song leader returned to center stage and led us in the hymn that often closed the service. The words tell the story all by themselves:

> I was sinking deep in sin,
> Far from the peaceful shore,
> Very deeply stained within,
> Sinking to rise no more;
> But the Master of the Sea
> Heard my despairing cry,
> From the waters lifted me,
> Now safe am I.
>
> Love lifted me, love lifted me,
> When nothing else could help,
> Love lifted me.

The song leader used to prolong that last line by extending his left arm upward, as if pointing up to heaven. The effect was powerful. Our hearts really did feel uplifted.

Once the singing had subsided, the chapel emptied quickly into the welcome cool of the Missouri evening. Tables were set up with generous slices of cellar-cooled watermelon, and soon their seeds were splattering the lawn like oversize drops of rain. Women clustered and gossiped. Men engaged in farm talk. Teenage boys and girls stole shy glances, and we departed, eager for the next day's uplifting evening, which is why they were called revival meetings. They were intended to revive our very spirits, and they did.

COLLEGE!

By 1936 I had chosen Central College as my landing pad in America, and I would attend this school for the next four years with the best of intentions to follow in my father's footsteps and become a missionary. I found the arrival exciting. Never mind that the school's total enrollment was six hundred and that it was situated in Fayette, Missouri, population three thousand. Compared with my Podunk hometown in China, which I could walk across, Fayette was bright lights, big time: the Big Apple to me. No narrow cobblestone lanes here. The streets were wide and *paved*, and almost every family owned an automobile. The town square was lined with shops that sold everything one's heart could desire — clothing, watches, jewelry. You name it, you could buy it. Though families usually ate at home, there was even a small restaurant, where — as I learned when I sought the company of girls — a dime would buy lemonade for two. There was also a motion picture theater in which a film was screened every Saturday! I had seen *one* movie theater in China in the seventeen years I had lived there, and that was when my parents took me to Shanghai to see

The Iron Horse. This was the film where the director had dug a pit under the railroad ties and filmed while the train raced over the camera. I had never seen simulation before, so I wasn't prepared for that shock. I remember ducking under my seat to save my life!

Saturday-night films in Fayette were a world apart. When we arrived at the cinema we would approach the proprietor, dressed in a tuxedo in his dingy booth, and we would push a quarter through a slot in the window for a ticket. He would then emerge from the booth and walk to the door of the theater and tear our tickets in two. I don't remember any names of the movies I saw in those days. It doesn't matter — I had already seen *The Iron Horse.* I had seen the best!

THE SPARK OF LEARNING

Still, it was the college that was the center of my excitement. By national standards it was nondescript, humdrum, no great shakes. But the college offered two great teachers — and they were professors of philosophy and religion. But *that's all it takes* to inspire a willing student. One of them I remember well and am grateful to him to this day. Edwin Ruthven Walker by name, professor of philosophy and religion, held me spellbound, and like every great teacher, he inspired me to think for myself, and more, to think well of my own capabilities — and then to use them.

One day he opened the class session by saying, "Last night I read three sentences that were as inspiring as any I can recall." My heart leaped to my throat as I heard him reading words that I had written in a recent paper for his class. It is one of my first memories of sheer rejoicing.

I often feel sorry for today's college students, for the mega-universities have all but swallowed up colleges, and professors rarely know their students by name anymore. Central College was otherwise. Our professors lived across the street, and we were in and out of their houses all the time.

True to form, Professor Walker founded an honors society, which even boasted a Greek name — Phi Rho Kappa. It was essentially a philosophy of religion club, and its members consisted of the students who had earned As in Walker's courses on philosophy and/or religion. Every Thursday night we would meet in his home. We took turns writing three-page essays, and the evening was spent discussing the paper in question with the other honor students and our professor. Promptly at 10:00 p.m. Professor Walker's wife would arrive with cherry pie à la mode, which we eagerly wolfed down, and then we would adjourn.

I remember one of those evenings as being especially significant, even decisive, in my growth as a thinker. I would even consider it the first of two major epiphanies in my life. My excitement had been mounting throughout the evening's discussion, and it kept intensifying as our motley group of students made its way back to the dormitory. But we still couldn't stop talking, and so three or four of us clustered there in the hall, talking about the ideas that had come up during the evening's discussion, as unlikely a clutch of young peripatetic philosophers as one would find anywhere.

Finally, after what seemed like hours of intense talk, we realized that we had to get some sleep if we were to make our eight o'clock classes the next morning. So we dispersed and went to our rooms.

But my mind kept churning.

I tried to go to bed, turning out the light in hope of some rest. Sleep, though, was out of the question. My mind kept racing until around 2:00 a.m.

Then it detonated.

I was catapulted into an altogether different state of consciousness. My whole life seemed to unroll before me. Years later, I was reminded of this shift of consciousness when viewing the famous scroll that appears at the beginning of *Star Wars*.

I don't know if I slept a wink that night.

Decades later, when I was in the mountains of northern Mexico with a group of *peyoteros*, I participated in a series of prayer meetings in which I took some entheogens (psychoactive substances that awaken the divine spirit), which also catapulted me into a radically different state. But the state of consciousness I was transported to that night in my college dorm in Fayette was totally different. I don't know what to call the state of my mind that night — it wasn't mystical — but I will try to describe it here.

In this state it was as if I was *seeing ideas* as Platonic archetypes, and the seeing, the vision, was so electric that it felt as if my mind was going to explode.

When I arose the next morning for class I knew I wasn't going to be a minister. My vocation was set. Having already changed my aspiration from being a missionary to being a cleric, I now changed my mind again, this time to being a professor. At that moment of my epiphany I knew the world of the ministry wasn't for me. I needed to become a professor, a teacher, and live in the world of *ideas* because it was ideas that gave me joy. That is when I knew for the first time that I had to live in this world of teachers and thinkers, not the world of ministers and preachers. They had responsibilities and rules to follow, as I knew from being the child of one. That night in my dormitory I realized that being a professor would offer me the greatest opportunity to work with ideas.

CAMPUS ACTIVITIES

My college life wasn't all work. It did have a more playful side to it, which consisted of a remarkably wide range of exciting campus activities that helped me channel my youthful energy.

For I was ambitious, and I even wanted to become *famous*, a formidable word for a small college campus. But the idea pertains. In the phrase that was current then, I wanted to become "BMOC," the Big Man on Campus. That required getting to be known, and I decided that the best way to become known was to join as many organizations as possible. So I joined every club on campus, from the Scribbler's Club for fledgling writers, to the Glee Club for songsters, to the Debaters for those who wanted to practice skills that would be useful if they became lawyers. You name it, I joined it.

The strategy paid off. Sequentially, I was elected president of the freshman, sophomore, and junior classes, and student body president in my senior year. I almost forgot to mention that I edited the student newspaper along the way.

It is ironic, but true. Activities took precedence in my first two years, but when *ideas* took over, I spent my last two years getting out of all the activities I had signed up for in my first two years.

Chapter Three

Launching My Career

The night of my epiphany determined my vocation. But in order to realize my dream of becoming a professor, I needed to steep myself more in the world of academics.

So I entered the University of Chicago, in 1944, to complete my postgraduate work. It proved to be the ideal time to enter that vocation, despite the admission by its chancellor, Robert Maynard Hutchins, "It's not a very good university; it's just the best there is." I had earned my PhD (the union card for teaching), World War II had ended, and returning GIs were flooding college campuses on the GI Bill, which allowed them to continue their education.

By the time I had earned my doctorate, in 1945, the atmosphere was propitious for teaching. I was offered a position at Denver University, and that's where my career as a professor began.

To succeed, now as then, professors need three things. First, professors need to know their stuff, what they intend to teach their students. Second, they need to know how to communicate, how to get what they know into the minds of their students, skillful communication being the essence of good teaching. Third, if professors are to rise in their profession they must be able to write books to contribute to the sum of human knowledge. Of those three, I knew my subject matter reasonably well. But I do not consider myself a scholar — there are innumerable professors who are better scholars than I am. I will speak to writing later. But for now I want to talk about what I consider my chief forte, namely, *communication.*

There is objective evidence here. My book *Why Religion Matters: The Fate of the Human Spirit in an Age of Disbelief* received the Religious Communicators Wilbur Award in 2001 for being the religious book that best got the word across to the general public about the true importance of spiritual matters.

COMMUNICATING IN A THIRD-GRADE CLASSROOM

To illustrate how I have been able to effectively communicate ideas about religion, I would like to recount a memorable encounter that happened several decades ago. One day I received a letter written in pencil — the only letter I have ever received in pencil, incidentally. It read as follows, all in a child's handwriting:

Mister Smith.

We are studying religion. We do not know religion. Will you tell us about religion?

— The third grade

Now, truth to tell, I receive more invitations to speak in public than I would like, but this one was different, and it intrigued me. A phone number was penned in, so I called it and arranged for a time for me to come to the designated classroom.

When I knocked on the classroom door a few days later, I was greeted by a blast of energy that almost knocked me off my feet. Neither the teacher nor I had thought ahead about the class time, which was the last class session of the week. So we weren't prepared for how jazzed the pupils were and the way they were champing at the bit to get into their weekends.

What to do? Providentially, inspiration hit me.

Don't try to *talk* to these kids, I said to myself. Nothing you say will get through to them. They need *action*. So I seated myself on the table and said, "You asked me to come and *tell* you about religion, but I'm not going to tell you about religion. I'm going to teach you to do religion."

Mounting attention.

"Have any of you heard of Japan?" I asked the class.

Arms waving everywhere.

"Good, because I'm going to teach you to do religion the way they do religion in Japan."

Riveted attention.

"When they do religion in Japan, they sit on the floor," I told them. "So, everybody get up and push your desks against the wall."

Great glee! The youngsters pushed their desks toward the walls, intentionally bumping into one another, as kids will do when they are excited. Finally there was an open space in the middle of the floor, and the kids were sitting in it.

"Good," I said. "Now, when they do religion in Japan, sitting on the floor like you are doing, they sit in a special position."

With that simple introduction I assumed the full-lotus position right on top of the teacher's desk.

"Can you sit this way?" I asked them.

Several show-offs proceeded to copy me, beaming proudly as they did their version of the lotus position.

"Good," I commended them.

Then, so the other students wouldn't feel inferior, I added that the special position wasn't that important. Sitting cross-legged would be just fine.

"Now," I continued, "when the Japanese do religion they sit very still, not moving their bodies at all. Can you do that?"

Vigorous nods all around the room.

"For fifteen minutes," one little voice sang out.

"Can you *really* sit for fifteen minutes, without moving at all?" I asked again.

"Five minutes," came a voice from a distant corner.

We finally whittled down the challenge to two minutes, but even that was too long, for the young students all soon broke into giggles.

I glanced at the teacher, and she nodded. I continued, "Now you know how they do religion in Japan! Class dismissed! Enjoy your weekend!"

There was sheer pandemonium as the kids rushed for the door. However, one little boy suddenly stopped and asked me if I liked jelly beans. I said, "I sure do! Especially *black* jelly beans!" The boy reached into a bag of jelly beans in his satchel and picked out all the black ones and put them into my hand.

The following week I received in the mail a small packet of black jelly beans, the sweetest and most touching honorarium I have ever received for a talk.

That experience reaffirmed my belief that religion is what we *do* with our spiritual life and our faith.

COMMUNICATING IN
THE COLLEGE CLASSROOM

When I began to teach at Denver University I couldn't believe
that I was being *paid* for doing something I enjoyed so much. Because my students responded, it was like a love affair between us.
My courses always attracted turn-away crowds, partly, I'm sure,
because I taught important material. The courses were world religions and philosophy, the big picture, but I taught that we can best
lead our lives in that context, with Socrates as the paradigm.

My large classes were so large, there was nothing I could do
but lecture and answer questions. However, there was always a
core of six or seven students who followed me to my office after
class. In some ways, that was where the real work of Socratic dialogue and discussion took place.

One of my students, George McClure, stands out for being the
spokesman for the group, but they all stayed until I said that I must
leave or I would miss the last bus from the campus, which dropped
me within walking distance of my home.

Call it an intellectual love affair, if you will, but it was a love
affair all the same.

Happiness! Rejoicing!

THE YOUNG WRITER

I remember the exact moment when I knew I could write publishable books. But truth in advertising matters. This is the one place
in this book where I wish to repeat a story that I related in a previous book, *Tales of Wonder*, and I ask the reader's indulgence in
allowing me to repeat the gist of it here.

While I was teaching at Washington University, in the early
1950s, to his surprise, a biologist named Tom Hall was appointed
dean of liberal arts, and he applied to the Carnegie Foundation

for a grant. This is the reason he gave: "I don't know what the humanities are about," he told us; "all I know is biology. I need to educate myself as to what the university should be teaching its students in the liberal arts."

Carnegie awarded him a grant for $18,000 to find out, a sum that meant much more back then. He then picked what he considered the best teacher in each department, and invited eight of the brightest young members of the faculty to meet in his apartment every other Sunday evening during the academic year to discuss the humanities and education. I remember reading a chapter from Cardinal Newman's *The Idea of a University*, and the philosopher Alfred North Whitehead's *The Aims of Education*. Hall took copious notes on what we said, and later he would throw the pages he had written on into a bushel basket by his feet.

On the last evening of our group meetings that academic year, Tom turned to me and said, "Huston, you are a bright young punk. You are scheduled to teach this summer, but I will relieve you. Instead of teaching, you should take this basket of notes and turn them into a report that I can send to the Carnegie Foundation to tell them what I did with their $18,000 grant."

When Kendra heard that I didn't have to teach that summer, she said, "Great, Huston, I've always wanted to visit Mexico. You can write your report from there."

Kendra and the girls and I targeted Santiago di Amendi as our landing pad because we had heard that it housed one of the most beautiful cathedrals in Mexico.

Kendra and I sat down and calculated that it would take a week to get there, so we pocketed seven twenty dollar bills, figuring that one of them would cover our expenses for a day's food and lodging. I am an early-morning person, so I got up early and bundled Kendra and the three girls into the car and drove while they dozed. We were on schedule.

Beauty before intentions led us to this wonderful summer.

I took a peach crate, stood it upside down, and then placed my Remington typewriter on top of it. During the next several weeks I was very conscientious and worked from nine to five typing up all the notes while Kendra and the girls enjoyed Mexico.

When I returned to the campus I handed the report over to Tom, and he liked it enough to distribute it to the liberal arts faculty to provide the context of what they should be trying to accomplish in their teaching.

"These are our marching orders," he announced to everyone. "This is what we are going to do."

My duty was complete.

Some weeks later, I was walking across campus and encountered a professor of speech, who seized the moment and said, "Oh, Huston, nice to see you. I've been meaning to contact you. Remember that report you wrote that Dean Hall circulated? We're reading three paragraphs from that report in a choral reading course that I'm teaching this semester. The assigned pages begin with the last paragraph on page nineteen, in case you're interested to see what we have chosen."

Well, I *was* interested.

The thought of my committee report being intoned as art struck me as so bizarre that when I was back in my study I pulled out the report, turned to page nineteen, and started to read. What I discovered was a complete surprise!

"Hey, not bad!" I thought to myself, and then mused: "This is really quite good!"

What happened next sounds equally bizarre, but it's equally true.

One day in the office I saw a flyer lying on my desk announcing a book that Harper & Row had published. On impulse, I stuffed the report I had written into an envelope and shipped it off to the address on the flyer. Within a week, I received a reply saying that if my report could be expanded tenfold it was publishable. A contract was enclosed in the return envelope. Here I was, at the tender age of thirty-one, and already I had a book contract.

Following my marching orders, I expanded the report into a book that was published as *The Purposes of Higher Education*, and the reviews were favorable. The dean of the Harvard School of Education rated it above the so-called *Red Book*, a thick tome that the Harvard faculty had taken two years to hammer out, to indicate what *it* intended to accomplish in its undergraduate curriculum.

And so it transpired that in my early thirties I had already met the third requirement for a successful professorial career. I could write publishable books.

When the book was published I traveled to New York and met my editor in a restaurant where editors and publishers gathered to talk about the world of books. I looked around and was bug-eyed: I had a glass of wine and my publisher had two martinis. I thought to myself, "So, this is how the other half lives!"

Chapter Four

Out of the Mouths of Babes

As a child our youngest daughter, Kimberly, answered to her middle name, Robin. One afternoon when she was three years old I was placed in charge of monitoring her afternoon nap. I bedded her down, but when I looked in on her after about an hour I found her standing up, holding on to the side of the crib, and looking so bright-eyed and bushy-tailed that I suspected the worst.

"Robin, did you go to sleep?"

There was a moment's pause for reflection, and then she said, "There's no answer to that question."

Struggling to keep the face of stern disciplinarian, I said, "Did you close your eyes?"

"There's no answer to that question, either."

Still sticking to the disciplinarian role, I ventured, "Robin, did you *lie down*?"

Immediately, she said, "There's no answer to that *kind* of question, either."

I gave up. She had bested me by catching me in what logicians would call a "category mistake." I had been barking up the wrong philosophical tree and asking categorically mistaken questions.

It was a lesson I would be able to use in the coming years as both a teacher and a writer.

Around the same time, we were invited to dinner at the home of friends, and Karen, our oldest daughter, was old enough for us to take her with us. The main wall of our friends' house was completely covered with Goya's painting of a voluptuous nude woman. On entering the room, Karen swept the wall with her eyes and then headed for its right-hand corner, where she placed her index finger on the part of women's anatomy she was most familiar with and announced: "Toes!"

One Sunday evening, when Robin was sleeping in a crib in a room of her own and had bedded down early, and Gael, our middle daughter, was sharing a double room with Karen, I overheard Karen say, "What's all this God business about? I don't get it."

Gael replied, "Oh, I do."

"No, you don't," said Karen. "You just *think* you get it."

"No, I really do," Gael protested. "I get some of it."

Karen, still incredulous and verging on contempt, said, "Like what?"

"Like God is in everything and does everything," said Gael confidently. "Like, I'm not dancing now; it's God dancing through me."

Resisting the knee-jerk impulse to shout, "Gael, you get back in bed this minute!" I asked myself, "What hope is there for the stern disciplinarian?" and decided to let it pass. I figured she would climb back into bed, go to sleep, and be none the worse for her brief escapade.

Another time our family had been singing a song that contained the line "Laura was a pretty girl, God almighty knows." When we finished the song we were ready to move on to other matters, but Gael wasn't done. Pondering thoughtfully for a moment she said, "How could she have been pretty when she had a *mighty nose?*"

When Karen was five years old she was sitting on the living room floor playing with her toys when Kendra told her to pick them up, telling her that it was suppertime. Karen responded with a deep sigh, "Why do I have to do everything before I can do anything?"

That sounds as if it hides a contradiction, but actually it makes perfect sense. I often find myself echoing her thought without voicing her words. For obviously what she was complaining about was having to do things she didn't want to do before she could do what she did want to do.

That resonates with me completely. Sometimes it sounds like the story of my life.

SIERRA

In the blink of an eye Karen had grown up, married, and given birth to a lovely baby girl, our first grandchild, Robin, who later switched to using her middle name, Sierra. One evening when Sierra was very young she visited us. I took her to the university theater, where a traveling theatrical troupe was staging a program of classical Indian dance. She wasn't interested; she wanted to go to a classroom where I taught.

Very touched by her request I led her through the twilight to a building on the University of California campus where I taught one of my classes in world religions. When we entered the classroom I turned on the lights. Sierra gazed at its vastness and then went to the blackboard, where she took a piece of chalk and printed her name: SIERRA.

"Now they will think I'm a student here," she said.

The following evening my seminar for graduate students met in our home. Sierra was so fascinated that she listened to and kept peeking in on the entire session through a crack in the door that opened onto the back stairs.

When the seminar concluded and I went upstairs, Sierra was waiting for me at her bedroom door.

"Oh, how I wish I were in college," she said, and through the burst of tears that followed, "and I'm only in first grade."

All the pathos of the universe poured through the cloudburst of tears through which those words were spoken.

ANTONIO

One day as I was playing with our grandson, Antonio, on the floor my eyes began to droop and I said, "I'm going to take a short nap. If I'm not up in ten minutes you can wake me."

It so happened that what I had expected to be a simple cat-nap turned out to be a solid hour of sleep. When I woke up I saw Kimberly's car entering our driveway and Antonio rushing out to meet her shouting, "Mom, has it been ten minutes since a long time ago?"

I would like to share a few more incidents about the delightful wisdom of children before bringing this short chapter to a close. One incident feels suspended in midair because I cannot recall exactly *when* the incident occurred (in time) or *where* it occurred (in space). So it feels timeless. However, the incident is so vividly imprinted on my mind that I can visualize it even to this day.

Years ago, a neighborhood boy around four years old would cross our quiet street after his supper and take my hand, and we would walk together around the block. I would begin our conversation by telling him what I had been doing, and at every pause he would say, "Den what?"

One evening, I decided to reverse the roles and ask *him* what *he* had been doing, and again at every pause I would ask him, "Den what?" After four or five of those queries, he stopped in his tracks and looked up at me, saying to me sharply, "No more den whats!"

And now a few more short tales to tell. This curious question was addressed by a three-year-old boy to a grocery store clerk, who was checking out his mother's purchases. As he passed the candy rack, the boy stuffed all his pockets and both hands with as much candy as he could manage. He was in hog heaven. However, one item of candy was still missing, and he felt he needed to report it: "Has you got any lollipops?"

Those of us who were standing behind them had to wait while the boy's mother returned all her son's loot to its proper place.

I can't resist a final gem from the mouths of babes.

One April Fools' Day, a friend of ours handed his son an ice-cream cone filled with mashed potatoes. "How do you like it, son?" he asked. "Oh, it's good! I like it all right. But it does taste a little like mashed potatoes."

Curiously, I often think of that reply when I'm asked to endorse so-so books. "It's an okay book," I'm tempted to write, "but it *does* read a little like mashed potatoes."

Chapter Five

Being Driven Temporarily Psychotic in Kyoto's Temple of the Marvelous Mind

I n the mid 1950s, I was drawn to Buddhism through D. T. Suzuki, whose writings, such as *Manual of Zen Buddhism* and *An Introduction to Zen Buddhism* (coauthored with Carl Jung), held out the prospect that Zen practice would offer at least a taste of satori, the enlightenment experience. I was in my midthirties, and at that age I wanted a taste of enlightenment more than anything else in the world — so much so that my friends charged me with "whoring after the Infinite." One could ask if there is any better whoring, but in any case it led to a summer of Zen training in Kyoto under one of the two Zen masters, or roshis, who at that time could not speak a word of English.

I knew that Zen practitioners sat in the full-lotus position, so when I decided to spend the following summer practicing Zen in

Japan, I knew I needed to break my legs in so I could sit in that position.

This proved to be an ordeal.

When I sat "witty right leg," thigh and shin on the floor, my left thigh slanted upward like a television aerial. Obviously some tendon stretching was required, so I set to work. My desk had eight-inch-long legs, so I began ramming my left knee under its drawer. After a week or so of stretching my tendons, I wedged a thin pamphlet over my knee to force it down further. Every week I continued that regimen, increasing the width of the pamphlet until it attained the width of a book. By this torturous method, when I was ready to leave for Japan I had succeeded in stretching my right leg tendons until I could sit full-lotus on the floor.

Before proceeding with my story, I will interrupt it with a moment of whimsy. Once, in a television course on world religion that I was giving, I described the full-lotus position and assumed it on the table I had been leaning on in the studio. The action drew a response written on a note card that was folded and sealed with Scotch tape. The note read:

Dear Professor Smith:

This will not be long, for I can't write well in this position. I have my right foot in my left pocket, and my left foot pretzelled and resting on my right thigh. My question is: How do I unwind? I am eagerly awaiting your next program.

Yours truly,

A fan

Now let me fast-forward.

When the 1955–1956 academic year ended, I flew to Japan to enter Zen training with Zen Master Hiroshi. During the months that I was "breaking my legs in," I would go on Tuesday evenings to sit with a small Zen group in Cambridge. By a route that I will not trouble the reader by describing, the leader of that group put me in touch with her mentor, Ruth Fuller Sasaki (she had married her Japanese Zen master to keep him from being drafted into the army during World War II), who had been training for many years in Kyoto under one of the two roshis who had led a small Zen group in Los Angeles for two years.

Mrs. Sasaki had set things up for this step of mine, so I was met at the Tokyo airport and driven to her home. I rested there for a day or two, and then she took me to Myoshinjisodo, to introduce me to the roshi under whom I would train. To spell things out a bit, *ji* means "temple" and *sodo* means "monastery," while *Myoshinji* is translated as "marvelous mind." Pieced together, this comes out rather poetically as "the Monastery in the Temple of the Marvelous Mind."

When Mrs. Sasaki left, I was alone with my roshi in his audience chamber. He introduced himself as Goto Zuigan Roshi and said he understood that I wanted to enter Zen training. When I concurred, he said that in Zen we sit in a special position, wherewith he lifted his ceremonial robe and revealed the full-lotus position he was sitting in.

"Can you sit this way?" he asked.

When I forced my legs into the lotus position, he grunted, which I took as a sign of at least grudging approval. Then he asked me, "How long can you sit in this position?"

Now, I knew that there were two branches of Zen, and that in *soto* the monks would break for five minutes of walking meditation every forty minutes. In *rinzai*, they would break for walking meditation every twenty-five minutes. I also knew that my roshi was in the *rinzai* school, so I said that if I could break every twenty-five minutes for walking meditation, I assumed that I could sit that way forever.

I lived to rue those words.

"There's an empty room next to this one," he said. "You can go in there, and we will see how it goes."

It went very badly. I had never tried to sit in the lotus position forever. Truth to tell, I had only sat in it for a twenty-five-minute session at the start of each day.

The first session in the empty room and the five-minute break went all right, but none of the others did. I quickly learned that leg tendons do not fully relax in five minutes. This meant that in each subsequent twenty-five-minute period I began with a handicap, and those handicaps built up exponentially. As the weeks of sitting progressed, the pain gradually diminished, but in the ten weeks of sitting the discomfort never completely disappeared.

THE USE OF ZEN KOANS

If one wants to understand the wholeness and interconnectedness of life, Zen teaches, it must be viewed from many perspectives. Goto Roshi's branch of Zen uses koans, which translate as "problems," to help us do this. Koans are intended to help the practitioner solve spiritual riddles.

There are many different kinds of koans. The beginner koans are rather like shaggy-dog stories, in that they pose questions, riddles, really, that make no rational sense, such as the classic "What was the appearance of your face before your ancestors were born?" Another classic koan is "What is the sound of one hand clapping?" If you answer by slapping one hand in the air against an imaginary hand, you are likely to get a sharp rap on your skull with a hardwood stick (about nine inches long with a convoluted end), which roshis keep at their sides to deal with stupid answers.

The koan I was given was longer than most. In Tang dynasty

China, a monk asked a famous master named Joshu, "Does a dog have a Buddha nature?" To which Joshu replied, "*Mu.*" His mysterious answer was "a kind of negative," my roshi informed me. Now, I knew that the Buddha had said that even the grass has a Buddha nature, so with that I had my koan, my problem. For how can a dog *not* have a Buddha nature when even grass has it?

For two agonizing months I banged my head against that contradiction all day long. Twice a day I had *sanzen* — a private interview — with my roshi. In those interviews I was to tell the roshi the answer to the conundrum he had given me.

Knowing of no other way to proceed, I attacked my program rationally. But how does one iron out a contradiction? Well, you fiddle with the terms and redefine them. Perhaps the dog wasn't a genuine dog, or maybe it was only a part of a dog that didn't have a Buddha nature, and other such far-fetched explanations. Obviously, I was grasping at straws.

After my first far-fetched answer, Hiroshi simply rang the little bell that he kept by his mat, which signified that the interview was over. But after a couple of days of *ting-a-linging* he became vocal.

"You have the philosopher's disease," he shouted.

Seeing that his sudden shouting set me back on my heels and left me somewhat stunned, he changed his tone of voice.

"You're a philosopher," he said. "There's nothing wrong with philosophy. I myself have a master's degree in philosophy from one of our better universities here in Japan. But philosophy works only with reason. There's nothing wrong with reason, either; it's very useful. However, reason can only work with the experience it has at its disposal. You obviously have the reason, but your experience is limited. Use these weeks as an opportunity to enlarge your experience, and your teaching will be different again."

Ting-a-ling.

So there I was, sitting in the cramped lotus position all day long, knocking my brains out against that absurd koan and twice a day reporting one-on-one to my roshi what I had come up with — which was precious little! I seemed to be getting nowhere, though I did discover as the weeks dragged by that the final word in the koan, *mu*, seemed to be functioning more and more like the *om* mantra that I had worked with in Vedanta (a branch of Hindu philosophy).

FINAL EXAMINATION

Zen monasteries have two three-month terms, one in the summer, one in the winter. In the spring, the monks return to their homes to help their families plant rice, and they return in the fall to help them harvest it.

The last week of each term is a kind of final-examination period during which work in the garden is suspended. Zen monks try to be self-supporting to allow the monks to meditate around the clock. I was told that some of the monks did do that and never lay down. They caught what catnaps they could when the *jikijitsu* (a kind of sergeant at arms who patrolled the meditation hall) wasn't looking.

For that final week of the term, Goto Roshi acceded to my request to be admitted to the monastery. This was noteworthy because Myoshinji is said to be the strictest of all the Zen monasteries and had never admitted a Westerner. Later, it was reported that one foreigner was admitted after me, but he didn't stick it out, and that was the end of the line for foreigners at Myoshinji.

I was a novice, and at thirty-seven I was also the oldest of the aspirants, who were in their early twenties. So I was permitted to sleep three and a half hours each night of that final-exam week, which I found grossly insufficient. After the first night I was simply sleepy. After the second night, I was bushed, and it got incrementally worse. There was nothing to do but to simply take it from there.

Being Driven Temporarily Psychotic in Kyoto's Temple

After all this time and all my studies, I still don't really understand how Zen training works. Zen masters can come across as being as slippery as greased pigs, but they can also be solicitous and nurturing in the way they assist their students in reaching satori, reminiscent of Jacob's ladder as described in the Christian hymn:

> We are climbing Jacob's ladder,
> We are climbing Jacob's ladder,
> We are climbing Jacob's ladder,
> Soldiers of the cross.

> Every rung goes higher, higher,
> Every rung goes higher, higher,
> Every rung goes higher, higher,
> Soldiers of the cross.

Nevertheless, it seems clear to me now that the initial koan is designed to force the rational mind to the end of its tether, and that sleep deprivation comes in somewhere along the line. If you can't get your mind into an altered state by meditating, sleep deprivation will eventually do the job for you, for sleep deprivation increases serotonin, a neural transmitter, and that increases the probability of hallucination. Denied the opportunity of dreaming while we are asleep, we will dream while we are awake, which amounts to a kind of temporary psychosis.

Something like that happened to me two days before the final-exam period ended. During those eight days we had private audiences with the roshi, twice a day, at five in the morning and at two in the afternoon. On the sixth day of the eight-day intensive I went storming in to my roshi in a fury. Self-pity had long ago become boring; now it was anger, undiluted rage. I was furious. What a way to treat human beings, I kept telling myself, as I charged in. Although I had come to revere my roshi I was prepared not just to throw in the towel but to smack him across the face with it.

Despite my anger, I entered his audience room in the required ritualistic manner. Palms clasped together I bowed, supposedly reverentially, and approached the roshi along the walls of the room, making only right-angle turns. You don't cut corners in Zen!

When I reached him where he was sitting in his priestly robes I noticed he had his short "clobber stick" in his lap just in case he needed it. I sank to my knees on the pad before him and touched my head to the tatami mat. Then I flexed my outreached fingers upward to symbolize lifting the dust off the feet of the Buddha. I sat back on my haunches, and our eyes met in a mutual glare. I waited for him to speak. For a few moments he said nothing, and then he growled, "How's it going?" It sounded like a taunt.

"Terrible!" I shouted.

"You think you are going to be sick, don't you?" Since he was resorting to more taunting sarcasm, I let him have it.

"Yes, I think I'm going to be sick!" I yelled back.

For several days my throat had begun to contract, and I was having to labor to breathe.

And then the miracle happened. His face relaxed; his taunting, goading expression disappeared, and with total matter-of-factness he said, "What is sickness? What is health? Put both aside and go forward."

I despair of being able to convey adequately the impact those twelve words had on me. Without reflecting, I found myself saying to myself, "By God, he's right!"

How he was able to spin me around, defuse my rage, and restore me to my right mind I shall never know. What I do know is that I have never felt so instantly reborn and energized. It was as if a pipe had been connected from his *hara* (the abdomen, where the Japanese locate the center of the body's energy) to mine and a transfusion was effected. I exited in the prescribed manner, not only determined to complete the two remaining days but confident that I could do so.

I later learned that in that climactic moment I had passed my koan, for it enabled me to experience — not just theoretically, but palpably — the *coniunctio oppositorum*, the identity of opposites. In my case, it was the identity of sickness and health, which are normally opposites. I had known that therapy requires the therapist to say exactly the right words at exactly the right time, but the way my roshi set things up still strikes me as genius. Get the patient's emotions aligned in the right way, give a light tap with the right words, and *ping*, the miracle happens. (Later, I came to see that my entire *life* has been a *coniunctio*, a putting together of opposites. Is it possible that *all* human life consists of a *coniunctio*?)

THE DENOUEMENT

I have not mentioned that Kendra was with me during that Japanese sojourn. We had rented a room with a small kitchen. One day, during the eight days that I resided in the monastery, Kendra came to the monastery entrance, hoping for at least a glimpse of me. She saw four chairs on the *ro'ku*, a narrow ledge that surrounds Japanese buildings, but she was turned away at the door. After I was back with her she showed me a quatrain she had written about that aborted visit:

> For news of you I went calling.
> Four chairs precisely sat,
> And in the evening sun
> Dust drifted down.

I also found a line that she had scribbled on an envelope: "I long to cling to you like a wet shirt."

The denouement of my strenuous "final exam" brought a final surprise. Through those eight days of sleep deprivation, I yearned for the moment when I could collapse beside Kendra on our futon and sleep around the clock — eight days in a Zen *sesshin* (extended meditation), followed by eight days in bed would give a nice symmetry to the experience, I thought. But I was dead wrong. I made manic love to Kendra for an hour before falling asleep.

But I do not want to end this depiction of my Zen training without returning to its sine qua non, my roshi.

As I was readying myself to return to America, he invited me to his tiny house on the temple grounds. He met me at its doorway dressed informally and welcomed me into his small living room. We did not sit down, for he said he wanted to show me the backdrop of his professional life. He introduced me in passing to a short, wizened woman working at a tiny stove on the other side of a short hanging curtain.

"This is Oksan, who takes care of my food," he said.

Then through more sawed-off curtains, he gestured to a futon on which a thin coverlet was spread. "This is my bedroom, and this is my television, where I watch sumo wrestling. Do you watch sumo wrestling? Oh, too bad. It's wonderful!" Then he led me out the back door, where boxes of empty beer bottles were stacked. "And here are the remnants of the beer I drink while I watch sumo wrestling."

We returned to his small living room and sat down. Obviously he had wanted to debrief me. He didn't want me to leave with him still on the pedestal where my veneration had placed him. He was kicking the pedestal out from under himself.

He then delivered a short homily on gratitude.

"You will be flying home tomorrow," he said. "Don't overlook how many people will help you get home — ticketing agents, pilots, cabin attendants, those who will have prepared your meals."

My roshi then placed his palms together and bowed in *gassho*, the gesture of gratitude. Straightening up, he pointed to the beam that supported the corner of the house we were sitting in. Another *gassho*. Looking up at the ceiling, he pointed out that it kept the house dry. Yet another *gassho*.

Then, turning his attention to me, he said, "Turn your whole life into an act of gratitude. I wish you a safe journey home and am glad that you came. Good-bye."

Chapter Six

Our Love Affair with the World

*Socrates thought it futile to catalogue the world
without first loving it.*

— BETTANY HUGHES, *The Hemlock*

The story of Kendra and my love affair with the world
begins with the story of a remarkable man. William H.
Danforth came of age at the height of the Great Depression, and figuring that as long as there were people, they would
have to eat, and as long as there were grazing animals such as cattle
they would be able to, he opened a small feed store on the banks
of the Mississippi River. Within a year, it burned to the ground.
Had it been me, I would have said so much for feed stores! But
Mr. Danforth took it as a sign that he should build a larger feed
store, which he did, turning it into Ralston Purina, one of the two
hundred largest corporations in America today.

During the corporation's tremendous years of growth, in the
mid-1950s, I was teaching a televised course on world religions.
One day I received a letter in the mail that read as follows:

Dear Mr. Smith,

I am following your television course and understand that some of the religions you are teaching about are in countries you have not visited. If you could arrange a semester's leave from teaching duties, I would be willing to underwrite a trip around the world for you and Mrs. Smith, but not for your children, for they would interfere with your research.

Sincerely yours,

William H. Danforth

Kendra and I were dumbfounded — and hamstrung! This was a once-in-a-lifetime opportunity, but what about our children? Kendra especially faced a dilemma. If she went on the trip she would hate herself for deserting our children, which numbered three at the time. But if she stayed with them, she would hate *them* for depriving her of experiencing the world. Although it was possibly an act of rationalization, she concluded that she would rather hate herself than our children, so she accompanied me on the journey.

That decided, things turned out very well. A couple we knew, who were very close and who had sons the same ages as our daughters, moved into and monitored our enlarged household. I can simply refer to the title of this book and say that the arrangement managed to leave everyone rejoicing.

In planning our trip, we almost decided to skip England and go straight to the Continent. Why, we asked ourselves, should we waste our time on a country that must be much like America, since it was English speaking? We couldn't have been more wrong! In its own way, as we were to discover, England is almost as different from the United States as any of the countries in continental Europe.

In 1956 there were no nonstop flights across the Atlantic, which necessitated our stopping at Gander, in Nova Scotia, to refuel. The entire trip took seventeen hours, and since we had left Chicago at midday we were already exhausted. By the time we reached our hotel in England it was midafternoon there, so we decided to take a nap before dinner but slept straight through. We awoke the next morning to the sounds of London: the ring of a man's leather-heeled shoes on the pavement, the clip-clop of a horse pulling a milk wagon. Then came the sound of a cornet in a small Salvation Army band. Looking out the window we could see their leader holding out a tambourine for passersby to toss coins into.

We took a day off to rest. The following morning at breakfast Kendra was reading *The Times* and noticed an article about a man who claimed not to have slept for forty-eight years. In those days I was so eager for life that I begrudged sleep for preventing me from getting on with all the things I was keen to get to. That meant I couldn't resist the temptation to meet this man and see if he had a secret I should know about. I told the hotel's concierge the name of the village where the sleepless man lived and asked if it was far away. He said a train ride to the village would only take about an hour. As if that weren't enough, he dug up the man's telephone number for me and even dialed the number and handed me the receiver. The sleepless man of local legend agreed to receive me.

Eustace Bennett was his name. He met me at the railroad station of his village, and we were no sooner seated in his small cottage than he told me his story. He was a retired farmer and had been born into a family of poor sleepers. Forty-eight years before we met, his sleep had deteriorated to the point where there came a night when he didn't lose consciousness at all. (I suspected, as he spoke, that he enjoyed some hours of twilight sleep, but I will let that pass.) The next night passed without sleep, and he became alarmed enough to consult the village physician, who monitored his vital signs for a week. Finding that they continued to be normal, the doctor concluded that the sleeplessness was a matter of brain chemistry. His advice to Eustace was for him to lie flat in bed for eight hours each night and continue with life as usual.

"Everyone has his own cross to bear," Eustace reflected. Sleeplessness was his, he told me. Often, after sitting by the fire at the end of a day's work in his fields, he would feel drowsy, and he would steal upstairs and lie in bed hoping that the miracle would happen. But as soon as lay down he was wide awake. Not one to construe the situation as his problem alone, he kept a telephone by his bed so that any of his neighbors who might also suffer from insomnia could call him, knowing he would be awake. This gesture, he said, of being available to others suffering from the same disability, was the one contribution he thought he could make to the world. He had discovered that there were at least four other people in the world who shared his affliction, and he corresponded with them.

I still have the photograph I took of him that day. He looks rather sleepy.

That visit wasn't only interesting but permanently cured me of my aversion to sleep. As I said, at that time in my life sleep seemed like a waste of time, and I went to great lengths to reduce its intrusion into my life.

For instance, while I was a graduate student at the University of Chicago, I read that people sleep most soundly during the first two hours after they go to bed. So my solution was to maximize those two-hour stretches instead of the standard single eight-hour stretch. I was able to attempt this because I had recently completed my course work and was preparing for my comprehensive examinations, which freed me to schedule my days as I wished.

However, the experiment failed, not for any physiological reasons but for a psychological one. At three in the morning I would take a break and go across the street, in South Chicago, for a cup of coffee at a lonely all-night delicatessen. The experience depressed me so much I gave up the experiment.

After meeting Eustace, I felt far less guilty about sleeping. The older I grow the more I cherish Elizabeth Barrett Browning's line "He giveth his beloved sleep."

OUR GRAND TOURS

Continuing eastward, Kendra and I crossed the English Channel into continental Europe. After viewing Notre Dame Cathedral and ascending the Eiffel Tower in Paris, we journeyed south, and in southern France we enjoyed the powerful aesthetic experience of viewing the seventeen-thousand-year-old cave paintings at Lascaux. The caves there are part of an enormous network that constitutes one of the wonders of the world. The caves plunge underground for nearly a mile and branch at the far end into narrow alcoves and crevices, and the height of their ceilings ranges from five to eight hundred feet.

Those figures are only quantitative. The caves' true marvel is qualitative. The paintings on their walls and ceilings are miraculous. They consist primarily of bison, stags, ibex, horses, and mammoths. Their execution is so remarkable that the viewer suspects that at any moment the animals portrayed might detach themselves from the surface of the walls and move toward — or away from — the viewer.

Curiously, a profound conservatism reigns in these caves. The paintings were created over seventeen to twenty millennia without the slightest suggestion of change or development. Conservatism in art may be one of the hallmarks of a stable civilization. If its denizens find their situations deeply satisfying, they see no need to alter it. Gazing transfixed at these paintings, I felt I was simultaneously in a womb and a tomb, a veritable sepulcher of art. It was the first time it occurred to me that painting could change, but it could not progress or improve.

The oft-quoted story goes that when Picasso emerged from one of the caves (the Altamira ones, which are in northern Spain) he remarked, "After Altamira, all is decadence." Other scholars claim he said, "They had everything we have." I suspect he was referring to such elements of art as perspective, but he could have added that they were already using it better than many of our artists do today.

In Toledo, Spain, we visited La Sinagogo de la Virgen Blanca, the Synagogue of the White Virgin, a synagogue that was turned into a church in 1492, the year that hundreds of thousands of Jews were expelled from Spain. When we finally did see the Alhambra on a later world tour, it surprised us with its transcendent architecture. Its arcades seemed to repose in perfect calm like the static equilibrium of a crystal, and its fountains transformed courtyards into oases of freshness.

In Rome, historical monuments of the Immortal City were so numerous that I wore out my knees visiting them and was forced to remain in our hotel for three frustrating days until I could walk comfortably again.

Nevertheless, I have some vivid memories of those walks, such as one up the Scala Santa, the long flight of steps that penitents used to climb on their knees; the Capuchin Church on the Via Veneto, where the bones of monks who had died were cleaned and arranged into strange works of art such as rosettes and decorative swans; and the church whose reliquary claimed to house the foreskin that was reputedly removed from Jesus at his circumcision.

One Sunday Kendra and I attended a high pontifical mass, where in the massive crush of people, my wallet was stolen. Later that week, on a Friday evening, we dined with a Catholic friend, who surprised us by ordering meat. Respectfully, we said, "We thought Catholics didn't eat meat on Fridays."

"Oh, that," he said, nonchalantly. "Papa [the pope] doesn't mind if I eat meat on Fridays. It's just a convention."

From Italy we traveled to Greece, and when we arrived at our hotel in Athens, around 10:00 p.m., it was a brilliant and inviting moonlit night. When we gazed out our hotel window, there it was, the Parthenon, looming over us. We felt beckoned by it and climbed up the switchback path of the Akropolis to reach it. Nowadays the Parthenon is heavily guarded and protected, but fifty years ago we were able to range freely among the ancient stones and columns and to muse about Greek history.

After our explorations of Greece's classical past, we were scheduled to fly to the Holy Land but were troubled by rumors that it had been closed to Americans because of the Suez Crisis, which had erupted on July 26, 1956.

Concerned, we met with the American ambassador in Athens to ask about the situation. As expected, he asked for our passports but then stunned us by stamping them both "INVALID FOR THE MIDDLE EAST." Then he casually sat back in his chair and said simply, "Now we can talk." Presumably able to speak freely, the ambassador said that negotiations were proceeding, but the situation was in flux. No one knew when the ban would be lifted. It might be tomorrow, he said, but then again it might be in several weeks.

Needless to say, we hated to miss the Holy Land so we decided to wait a few days. After cooling our heels for three days, however, we realized that we could waste a great deal of precious time waiting around in Athens, so we booked a flight, scheduled to leave the next day, for Baghdad. We were actually boarding our flight, walking along the runway to our plane at the Athens airport, when a man came out of the terminal shouting, "Mr. Smith! Mr. Smith! There is a telephone call for you."

Incredibly, it was the American ambassador on the line telling us that the ban on travel to the Holy Land had just been — dare I say — miraculously lifted. I demanded that our checked baggage be redeemed from the baggage compartment on the plane bound for Iraq, and fortunately the airline complied. With bags in hand, Kendra and I returned to our hotel and gratefully rearranged our itinerary.

Taking advantage of the sudden change in plans, we decided to work in a brief stop in Constantinople, now Istanbul, in Turkey, before proceeding to Israel. However, our flight to Istanbul was delayed, and it was one in the morning before we reached our hotel. Three hours later, Kendra woke me with a gesture that meant, "Listen, listen..."

I went over to the window, where only yards away a shadowy figure was circling a minaret calling to the faithful to come to prayer: "*Allah akhab,*" he intoned in Arabic. "Allah is most great. Come ye to prayer. Come ye to the good. The hour of prayer has come. Come ye to prayer."

That was the moment that Islam entered my world, permanently, as it turned out.

The next day was Sunday, so we went to the cathedral. It was winter, and everyone in the packed congregation seemed to have a severe cold. We couldn't even hear the liturgist for all the sneezing, wheezing, coughing, and nose blowing that were going on. When it came time for the Eucharist, the congregation formed a line that moved in a single file up to the archbishop to receive the sacrament. I got in line, and when it was almost my turn I noticed that it was a common-cup Eucharist. The officiant was dipping a spoon with a long handle into a chalice and bringing up a spoonful of mead. I was terrified at the prospect of closing my lips over a spoon that hundreds of people with colds had closed their lips over. When the spoon was placed in my mouth I couldn't bring myself to close my lips until the officiant closed his teeth several times to signal to me to get on with it, for I was holding up the line.

I complied.

Still frightened at the prospect of catching pneumonia or the flu, I took Kendra's hand and together we raced from the cathedral back to the hotel, where we headed straight for the bar. There, I downed a double brandy, my rationale being that alcohol was a disinfectant and might kill the germs from that Eucharistic spoon.

In retrospect, I realized that my science was way off, but the brandy did relieve me of my worry about catching the flu or worse, and I escaped scot-free.

THE HOLY LAND

In 1956 Jerusalem was still a very small town pocked by many open ruined lots, owing to recent bombings. We stayed in the noted King David Hotel for a few days, then traveled on to an Orthodox kibbutz in the northernmost part of Israel. Our first day there, Kendra saw a rifle leaning in the corner of the living room, signaling the kibbutzniks' vulnerability to terrorists. The communal dining hall offered canned sardines, good brown bread, halva, and cucumbers and tomatoes from the gardens. Sunburned and exhausted men came in from the fields three times a day and ate silently.

After our visit to an Orthodox kibbutz we moved on to one ruled by Marxist philosophy, which meant there were no formal religious rituals and no private property, and the children lived in dormitories, separate from their parents. Since we were close to the border, the surrounding barbed-wire fence was accessorized with guard dogs on chains.

Since we had expressed our desire to travel on to Egypt after our stay in Israel, the Israeli customs officials stapled their official documents, which we could remove later, to our passports. They reminded us that evidence showing we had been in Israel would prevent our entry into Egypt.

Curiously, rather than facing suspicion when we entered Cairo, we were heartily welcomed. The reason was that we were the first foreigners to arrive in Egypt after the Suez Crisis had passed. We spent a day sightseeing along the Nile, visiting the Sphinx and the pyramids, and then running for a bus to take us back to our hotel. It turned out to be a school bus filled with children, but the driver obligingly drove us to our hotel. It was Ramadan. A professor who had visited Washington University at my invitation asked us to share his family feast after sunset.

When I consider my time in Cairo I recall a dear friend, Gray Henry, whose family home is outside Louisville, Kentucky. She married a Muslim and lived for thirty years in Cairo, becoming fluent in Arabic. Eventually, she and her husband separated and she returned home. A few years after the separation she returned to Cairo to visit friends. When she hailed a taxi from the airport she was so tired · from her journey that she failed to negotiate the fare, as is the custom there. When they arrived at her hotel the driver named his price.

I must now insert some context for the episode I am describing. As is well known, Muslims pray five times a day. The first time is when a white thread can be distinguished from a black thread, or when one awakens in the morning. Thereafter Muslims pray at noon, in late afternoon, at sunset, and before retiring. These five prayers ring the changes with a single component that consists of eight lines:

> Praise be to Allah, Creator of the worlds;
> The Merciful, the Compassionate;
> Ruler of the Day of Judgment.
> Thee do we worship, and Thee do we ask for aid.
> Guide us on the Straight Path,
> The path of those who worship Thee.
> Not the path of those who have incurred Thy wrath
> And have gone astray.

Now back to my friend caught in her dilemma in Cairo. She boldly told the taxi driver — in fluent Arabic — that she had lived there for thirty years and knew that the price he was demanding was an outrageous sum. The driver thought he had her where he wanted her, having already driven the long distance from the airport, and he claimed he wasn't backing down.

My friend said calmly, "All right. You and I both know that you are holding me up, but it is late and I am tired, and I see that you refuse to negotiate. So here is your money. But I want to say one more thing: Remember the Day of Judgment!"

The taxi driver's hands trembled. "Oh, the Day of Judgment, the Day of Judgment!" he cried. "Please keep your money. The ride is free!"

SOUTHEAST ASIA

In Burma, now called Myanmar, I sought out the United States cultural attaché to ask how he would recommend that we spend our few days there. He was an African American man who was on a two-year leave from the Harvard Divinity School, where he taught the New Testament. He urged us to prolong our stay by taking a ten-day meditation course taught by Sayagyi U Ba Kin. When he had taken the course, it had climaxed for him in a direct experience of Christ, which his education at Harvard had not afforded him.

Persuaded by his recommendation, we delayed our departure and enrolled in the course. I started immediately, but Kendra was convalescing from a bout with the flu and joined me later. Though I did not attain the hoped-for revelation, I do not regret the ten-day course.

The temple where the course was held was circular and divided into pie-shaped cells that had doors through which we entered and windows with shutters that opened onto the center of the "pie," where our guru sat. We could tap on those shutters if we had questions about our meditation, or he could open them from his side if he wanted to check on us.

For eighteen hours each day we sat on sleeping bags and tried to meditate. At 10:00 p.m. each evening we were allowed to sleep on the bags.

Unfortunately, the cell I was assigned to was too small for me to stretch out in. On the night before the course was to end, the guru took pity on me and invited me to sleep on a cot in his room. It turned out not to be the blessing he had intended. I spent the night getting up repeatedly and shaking out the sheet that covered me, which was solidly black from the ants that covered it. Meanwhile, the sheet under which the guru quietly snored was snow-white. Nary an ant could be seen.

Another tale of rejoicing because of its having been endured!

I learned from that encounter something my studies in the history of religion have repeatedly affirmed. My mentor required a female accomplice to empower him. Our guru was also highly educated and fluent in English, which was marked by an occasional oddity in phrasing.

To wit: whenever I went to him for advice, he would say, "It is an adventure, is not it?"

His accomplice, by contrast, was a poor, illiterate woman. However, she possessed the "divine eye," which in Buddhist iconography is placed in the middle of the forehead. She could see into the occult world, and he relied on her to instruct him as to how he should work with his devotees, since she could discern what was occurring in our psyches. One night, when the moon was full, our evening meditation was tabled while the Burmese people around us chanted praises and supplications to the deities that were hovering above our center. The divine eye could see them.

From Burma we flew to Japan and then back home. Our seven-month leave had expired.

Chapter Seven

A Globe-Circling Adventure

fter my first love affair with the world on our globe-circling adventure, the romance continued. Here in my writing I face a choice. Should I simply follow geography as Kendra and I circled the globe, or should I let time enter and report things that happened later on in these same places? Fearing that there might not be other places in this book to recount those later events, I am opting to honor geography rather than chronology. For example, in the early 1960s, I made a pilgrimage — not to Mecca, for I am not a Muslim, but to Konya, in the heart of Turkey. That is where the mystic philosopher-poet Mevlana Rumi poured forth his ecstatic poems while gyrating around a pillar in the local mosque. Over the next forty years I would travel around the world ten times, the highlights of which I shall try to collapse into a single narrative.

Our second around-the-world tour took place twelve years later, in 1969–1970. We began in Beirut, Lebanon, a crescent of a city with shining white buildings curving around a deep-blue Mediterranean bay. We flew there from Turkey and were delighted by what we encountered. Beirut was the cleanest and friendliest city we had yet visited and, in contrast to the cities we had visited in the early stages of our round-the-world tour, was undamaged by World War II. We were fortunate to be there at a time when America was loved everywhere. A portrait of John F. Kennedy was hanging on the wall of the barbershop where I got my haircut. The JFK half-dollars we handed out as tips were eagerly received. As modern as Beirut was, there was still ample evidence of its long history. Evidence of the Phoenician founders and its Roman settlers was everywhere, from the ruins to the old coins in the bazaar. Learning about the proximity of Byblos, the famed Phoenician port from which Egyptian papyrus was exported to Greece, we went up the coast to visit it. As is well known, our word *Bible* derives from *biblia*, meaning "book," which in turn derives from the seaport town Byblos.

After our travels around Lebanon, Kendra and I drove to Damascus, the capital of Syria, where the countryside lost its greenery and became more desertlike, and onward into Jordan. There we encountered a landscape studded with the black tents of desert nomads. Countless Bedouin men on donkeys were visible in the hills, driving their sheep, while Bedouin women in heavily embroidered black dresses took care of the camps. Their dresses, incidentally, later became popular in the American counterculture, brought back by the hippies who had traversed these same roads in the 1960s.

My most vivid memory is of staying in a beautiful hotel in an area that is now officially part of Syria. Since there was no official relationship between Jordan and Israel at that time, we could not legally take a bus or taxi from one country to the other. We had to walk across the border, carrying our suitcases through the Man-delbaum Gate. Our Jordanian driver watched sorrowfully as we deserted his beloved country for what he called "enemy territory."

ON TO INDIA

Days are never long enough for my visits to India. The exotic sights and sounds and smells completely captivate me. Early mornings and evenings in India are marked by the singular smell that arises from a half million cow-dung cooking fires drifting through the dust. It is a smell like no other in the world, and it is not pleasant. Still, I like it, perhaps because it assures me that I am in India.

When I was in the prime of youth I was manic during all my travels in India. I would charge around all day visiting places loaded with history and lore, and then sleep on a bus until I would wake up the next morning to repeat the routine. Invariably, several days later I would collapse and need to spend a couple of nights resting in a hotel.

Then, batteries recharged, I would resume my hectic routine. The poverty, the beggars, the dirt, and the squalor of the streets could not keep me from being happy, from rejoicing, for the name of God is in the very air of India, or at least it was in those days.

I could write a long chapter about my experiences in India, but I will limit myself to a few highlights.

In 1962 I was in Poona, where there is a center for the study of hatha yoga. When I visited I found two American scientists, one from UCLA and the other from the University of Michigan, who had been there for three weeks looking into the extravagant claims made by the practitioners of hatha yoga. When I asked them what they had found, they suggested that we step over to their neigh-boring cottage for tea.

Over traditional Indian tea they reported they had not found anything that, having seen it done, they could not explain. But they had found things that, had they not seen them done, they would not have believed *could* be done.

"Like what?" I had to ask.

"Well, there was this yogi," the scientist from UM said, "who claimed to be able to stop his heart from beating for the equivalent of five beats. When we wired him up with electrodes, he was wearing only a loincloth. The electrodes showed that his heart had not actually stopped beating. What he was doing was applying pressure at the point where the blood returns to the heart, so though the heart continued to beat it had no blood to pump."

The scientists told me that they had also compiled the data that they later published in a paper titled "The Metabolic Toll of the Headstand." Their conclusion was that standing on one's head "shakes the body up" more than any other position the body can assume.

In addition, I was informed through a story they passed on that when this particular yogi sensed that his time had come for him to "drop his body," as they say in Hindu circles, he managed to maneuver himself into the headstand position and collapsed, dead — at which point, one of his fellow yogis was reported to have remarked, "He always was a show-off."

On our 1969–1970 journey we visited the Taj Mahal in India, arguably the most perfect building ever built. It is a monument to love, a tribute by Shan Jahan, the fifth Mughal emperor, to his third wife, the princess Mumtaz Hahal, who had died shortly after their marriage. The Taj was begun in 1632 and completed in 1653. Not far away, in Delhi, is the Red Fort, which though it had had been built by the same emperor to house the royal family, ended up being used as a cantonment during the British period. Only its ruins now remain, but we were able to find the verse that he had chiseled on one of its walls:

If on earth there is a paradise of bliss, it is this, it is this, it is this.

THE KUMBH MELA FESTIVAL

The Kumbh Mela is the festival of the gods, one of the oldest festivals on earth, and by far the largest. Historians have been able to trace its beginnings back to at least 340 BCE, and its popularity continues to grow in our time, with upward of ten million pilgrims attending whenever the festival is held, which is, according to tradition, every twelve years. A Maha, or a Grand Kumbh Mela, which takes place in Allahabad, occurs every twelve times twelve, or 144, years, a cosmic number in Hindu metaphysics that symbolizes the turning over of an era.

It is recorded that in 643 CE, the Chinese Buddhist monk, scholar, and pilgrim Huan Tsang visited the Kumbh Mela in Allahabad (then known by its pre-Islamic name, Prayaga), and wrote, "The Mela is an 85-day-long assembly of wandering *sadhus*, *sannyasins*, and intellectuals, from all over India. Worship is offered to the Buddha, the Sun, and Shiva. Buddhist monks, Brahmins, and Jains receive gifts alike."

The festival is laden with mythic lore, including its location, which is in central India, at the convergence of India's three sacred rivers, the Ganges, the Yamuna, and the invisible Saraswati.

In 1977 I happened to be in the vicinity during the rarely held Maha Kumbh Mela, which attracted ten million devotees, and spent three weeks in utter fascination. It was an incredible spectacle. Pilgrims, spectators, media, and vendors came from all over the world. Gurus taught, *sadhus*, or Indian holy men, displayed their practices and peculiar powers, and attendees participated in elaborate processions. These spiritual parades were always highlighted by *nagas*, naked *sadhus* who have adopted the name of the sacred snake and who were granted pride of place at the head of the processions.

During my visit one guru boasted that he had the power to reduce his breathing to the point that the fuzz of a tiny feather held close to his nostrils could not be seen moving. He instructed his disciples to bury him in the sand with a surgical mask over his nose to keep out the sand, and further instructed them to release him three days later.

Unfortunately, on the first night the simple stick with a piece of cardboard nailed to it that was meant to mark the spot of the guru's burial blew away. The stick was never found; neither was the guru.

THE GOLDEN TEMPLE

Earlier I remarked on visiting the Taj Mahal during a previous trip around the world with my wife, Kendra. Here I will continue with the beautiful Gold Temple of the Sikhs, in Amritsar, India. Night and day someone can be seen waving the whisk of royalty over its sacred text, the Guru Granth Sahib, which Sikhs the world over regard as their living guru. Far from being a compendium of sectarian doctrines, the book consists entirely of divine poems by both Hindus and Muslims. I gladly cite from one of them here:

> Wonderful is sound.
> Wonderful is wisdom.
> Wonderful is life,
> Wonderful in its distinctions.
> Wonderful is praise.
> Wonderful is eulogy.
> Wonderful the presence
> One sees in the present.
> O, wonder-struck am I to see
> Wonder on wonder.

These hymns of praise for the one ineffable God formed the unifying vision of Guru Nanak, Sikhism's founder. Muslims and

Hindus alike revere him, and his message of interfaith understanding brought a sense of inner peace and calm to his country. Over Sikhism's three-hundred-year-long evolution, the Mughal Empire became less tolerant of the Hindu and Sikh communities, so the ninth Sikh, Tegh Bahadur, sacrificed himself to defend the rights of all people, Kashmiri Hindus in particular, so they might continue their way of life.

In response, Guru Gobind Singh, founder of the Order of the Pure (*Khalsa*), continued the mission to defend everyone's right to pray according to his own tradition without being persecuted.

To this day, Sikhs can still be identified by emblems of their faith, which include their turbans, beards, unshorn hair, steel bracelets, and small, symbolic daggers. For Sikhs, to cut one's hair, including body hair, is to disrespect what God has given us.

Wherever Sikhs worship, a communal kitchen is set up to feed all who wish to come, and its expense is borne by the entire Sikh community.

TEHRAN

Continuing east, we come to Tehran, the capital of Iran, where I'll begin with the extraordinary opportunity I had of attending in Tehran a *majlis*, a Sufi ceremony. For the times, this was an unheard-of opportunity. It was made possible by the most important Sufi in Iran. He had been a visiting professor at the Harvard Divinity School while I was teaching at MIT. I had sought him out, and we had become friends.

Back now in Tehran, he welcomed me to his country, and knowing that I was a pilgrim, not a tourist, he arranged for a companion to pick me up and take me to the *majlis*. Since Sufis are mystics who are not always appreciated by more exoteric, literal-minded Muslims, the *majlis* was held in the basement of a house that fronted onto an alley.

About forty of us arranged ourselves in concentric circles on the floor. There was no light except that which seeped through the transom of the wall facing the street. The Sufi chanting began, and I quickly noticed a change. The word *Allah* was replaced by the word *Ali*, signaling that I was in Shiite country. A brief explanation of this is in order.

The main division in Islam is between the Sunni majority and the Shiite minority. The split occurred in the first generation after Muhammad's death. The Prophet sired no son, and he did not appoint anyone to succeed him as leader of the Islamic community. Islam might have dissolved except for the line of able leaders, caliphs, who were elected by the Prophet's closest companions. Four Meccans who had been intimates of the Prophet collaborated to fill that role, but to avoid an interregnum, they appointed one of their number as interim titular head of Islam.

This is how the tragic Sunni-Shiite split began. One of the four, Ali, was a nephew of the Prophet, and the Sunnis believe that he should have been appointed the first of the four in the line of succession, whereas being the youngest he was last in line. This gives Shia the penitential air that I was witnessing in the *majlis* I was attending.

The chanting turned into wailing. As the fervor increased, bodies began to sway and heads began to flop from side to side. At one point I noticed someone across from me go into ecstatic spasms. Two "bouncers," as I retrospectively called them, for they were the largest of the men who had obviously been selected for this role, smothered the ecstatic in their arms until they calmed down.

After about forty more minutes, the wailing began to subside and then came to a halt. The circles regrouped into two lines facing each other. Swiftly and silently, a scroll of white paper was unfurled between the two lines. On top of it generous portions of couscous topped with raisins were dished out.

Those who had to work the next day departed after they had

finished their meal, but the old men lingered until dawn, I was told, to bathe in the lingering holy glow of the *majlis*.

ANGKOR WAT

Having avidly studied both Hinduism and Buddhism, I had always wanted to visit Cambodia, because it is home to the overwhelming majesty of Angkor Wat, the largest religious monument in the world. Built in the twelfth century, it is a testament to both religions. Its seventy-eight square miles of temples means it is the largest archaeological complex in existence, and yet only 2 percent of it has been excavated. One could wander for days and not take in all the iconography of Hinduism and Buddhism in its subtemples, statues, and images chiseled in still-beautiful bas-relief.

Roaming through the splendor of its ruins in the late 1970s, in blistering-hot weather, I was reminded of something in one of India's most beautiful temples, in Belur. The temple is richly carved. In its middle stands a column, on the back of which is a blank square. Under the square is written: "If anyone can find anything that I have not myself reproduced anywhere in my carvings he is at liberty to carve it here."

The space remains blank.

MEDITATING IN NEPAL

Early one morning, while I was meditating in a Tibetan monastery in Nepal, I sensed that someone had slipped in to occupy the vacant thin cushion to my right. I discovered that it was a woman when she leaned over and whispered in my ear, "Have you had breakfast?"

"I have had a *tsampa* barley ball and tea," I replied.

"Oh, go on," she said, laughing. "I'll feed you pancakes. See that building over there? My apartment is on the second floor, and I will leave a message on my door."

During my next stretch break I took the woman up on her offer and walked over to her apartment. There, I heard her amazing story. She had been the only woman magician with an international circuit. She had performed at Carnegie Hall, in Paris, in Berlin, and in Chicago, where before her appearance she needed to have her appendix removed. In those days they hospitalized such patients for a week, which is what happened with her. After her operation it took some time for her strength to finally return, and when it did she was bored lying there in the hospital. She looked around for something to read, but there was nothing but the Gideon Bible on her bed stand. The woman told me she had never even opened a Bible before, so she started at the beginning. She was immediately entranced.

"I even found the *begats* interesting," she told me. By the time she left the hospital her career had changed from magician to missionary.

Now, I come from missionary stock. But our missionary family was backstopped by the Board of Missions, from which we received monthly stipend checks. This ex-magician was without credentials. She explained, "I threw myself on the Lord," as she put it. And then she bought a one-way ticket to Nepal.

"How long have you been here?" I asked her.

"Two years," she said.

"How many converts have you made?"

"None."

Yet she seemed the happiest person in the world.

MOUNT ATHOS

One Easter, in 1975, I pilgrimaged to the holy Mount Athos, in northern Greece. Mount Athos is situated on a long, finger-thin peninsula that projects from Macedonia and climbs gradually for thirty-five miles until it drops precipitously into the Aegean Sea.

An inaccessible mountain crest separates it from the mainland. Its very lack of easy access and its natural beauty make it seem as if it doesn't belong to this world. Around the vast site are thickly wooded slopes that plunge straight into the sea, secluded coves, rocky headlands, and bays fringed by sandy beaches. Twenty monasteries that betoken long-gone centuries make it one of the most beautiful landscapes in the world. The glory of Mount Athos reflects the beauty of the Infinite, the place where heaven reaches down to touch the earth like the tip of a rainbow.

One of its oddest features is that people and supplies need to be hauled up from the sea to the monasteries above by winches, ropes, and large baskets. Another curiosity is that no females, not even female animals, are allowed on the grounds.

Nearby is a small city that services the monasteries, where tailors, shoemakers, shopkeepers, and the like help keep the monks going. When I visited, the small capitol had a strange feel about it. At first I thought that it was because there were no women, but then I realized, no, it was the absence of children. I had been in many places around the world where women were not permitted to be seen by strangers. But I had never been to a place that did not permit children. Never. It was very disconcerting.

But I had made the strenuous effort to come to Athos for a reason. I had long heard about the haunting liturgy that began at 2:00 a.m. on Easter morning and climaxed with the celebration of the Eucharist as the sun was rising.

It was a very moving experience. I rejoiced.

AN ENCOUNTER WITH ABORIGINAL AUSTRALIA

In 1961 I was invited to deliver the endowed Charles Strong lecture on world religions to a series of universities across Australia. The lecture tour took me on a wide swing from Brisbane, the country's easternmost city, all the way around the Australian coast to the westernmost city of Perth.

My professional duties were light. I delivered the same lecture at each of my stops. When I was asked how I would like to spend my spare time, I said I would like to spend it with the anthropologists at the universities where I was lecturing. I was eager to learn what they could tell me about Aboriginal culture. The ones I spoke with were unanimous in their conviction that the Aborigines have telepathic powers, surmising that *all* human beings have similar powers but that modern technologies, especially telephones and the postal service, had caused those powers to atrophy.

I was privileged to have several encounters with Aboriginal culture while in Australia. One time an anthropologist presented me with a beautiful bark painting of an emu. He explained to me that its painter belonged to the Emu Clan, and that the painting was meant to replace the emu that was prepared to sacrifice itself by allowing itself to be speared by him.

In Melbourne another anthropologist teamed me up for four days with a citified and cultured Aborigine who could speak English. The Aborigine led me into the bush, where he carved a boomerang. When he had perfected it, he threw it for about fifty yards, and when it flew back, as intended, it landed so close to his feet that he only needed to bend over to pick it up. (That very boomerang is mounted on the wall of my study, and I can see it as I write these lines.) My companion also honored me with tribal lore, but I was too sleepy to make coherent sense of the scraps I understood, and the rhythmic storytelling soon lulled me to sleep.

That same anthropologist asked me to carry to the Tiwi Aboriginals, on Melville Island, a copy of the *National Geographic* magazine that contained an article he had written about them. I was more than happy to oblige him, for I find it hard to say no to a looming adventure. Soon after, I flew to Darwin and arrived late in the evening and then contracted for a small plane to carry me the remaining few miles to the Tiwi Islands. The stationmaster met the plane and took me to his guest room. The next morning I was awakened by his angry yell, "Get the hell out of here!"

I opened my eyes just in time to see a kangaroo being ejected from my room by the stationmaster's swift kick in the pants, so to speak.

Thus chastened by the presence of wildlife on the island, I was taken by the stationmaster later that day to meet the local tribesmen. As soon as I opened the magazine to the spread that showed photographs of them they gathered around me eagerly to stare at the images. However, the excitement soon subsided when I innocently turned a page to reveal a photograph of one of the boys in the tribe. When their eyes fell on the picture, tears came pouring from their eyes, and they quickly covered their faces with their hands. The stationmaster quietly explained to me that the boy had recently died and the men were afraid that if evil spirits saw him they might occupy his body.

"They are also afraid," he added, "of the people sleeping inside the photographs."

THE BEAUTY OF BALI

In Bali I teamed up with a tourist from Jakarta who knew the local language. We rented bicycles and spent the days cycling through the beautiful countryside laced with rice paddies. At the northernmost point of the island we came across a lake and hired two boatmen to paddle us across. On reaching the far shore we were surprised by the rapid fall of darkness and were forced to spend the night in the traditional village that fished and cultivated a narrow strip of land at the foot of a mountain.

Owing to a culture that encourages and prides itself on its hospitality, we were welcomed and the villagers served us a delicious supper that consisted of freshly caught fish and freshly harvested rice. No outsiders had ever stayed overnight with them. After supper we were honored by being taken to a room where there was a double bed, the family's marital bed, we were told. All the men and boys who could crowd into the room did so to watch us undress down to our underwear. The villagers had never seen people in Western garb before, which made us as exotic to them as they were to us. Each item of clothing we discarded was passed around the room and examined carefully. Never, though, did we see a female during our entire visit. Occasionally, we heard whisperings behind the scenes.

For breakfast the next day, there was more rice and fish. Through my new friend and interpreter, I was able to ask some questions. Since they lived on such a thin strip of land, I wondered where they buried their dead. They didn't, I was told; they simply left the bodies exposed around a bend at the end of the strip of land.

The custom reminded me of the Tower of Silence, in Bombay, where the Parsee leave their dead for vultures to devour.

Our hosts were shocked when I told them about the Parsee.

"That is barbaric," they said.

"What is the difference between their custom and yours?" I asked.

"The Parsee corpses are prey to other creatures," they replied. "Our dead are disposed of themselves."

I didn't disturb them with the thought of maggots.

I can still recall the haunting strains of the boatmen's songs as they paddled us back to our bicycles.

For several days more, I lingered in Bali, even after my friend left. A throng of women chanting around a bungalow drew me up a hill to a tooth-filing ceremony, where a young marriageable woman was having her incisors filed to the same length. The room was crowded with women who, like the ones outside, were chanting loudly to show their support for the woman who was undergoing the ordeal.

When I reached my hotel I was told that since the moon would be full that night, there would be a festival, and it would be in walking distance. I couldn't resist and left after a short rest, reaching the festival site just as a gory cockfight was beginning. Around me vendors peddled various edibles. The dark night descended, which signaled an all-night performance of a melodrama based on the Ramayana. That book is one of the two great epics of India, the other being the Mahabharata, which contains the Bhagavad-Gita, one of the two most widely translated religious classics in the world, the other being the Taoist classic the Tao Te Ching.

To say that those two great Indian epics are huge is a vast understatement. Each narrative is more than twelve times the length of *The Iliad* and *The Odyssey* combined. The plethora of plots and subplots in the Ramayana is so immense that it is difficult to summarize it. Suffice it to say that the tale centers on the story of the god Rama's battle with and victory over Ravana, the ten-headed monster-demon who ruled Sri Lanka and abducted Sita, Rama's beautiful and virtuous wife.

This elaborate epic is endlessly resourceful and offers an inexhaustible treasure trove of melodramatic themes. The story swings back and forth from tears to boisterous laughter, and touches on every emotion between. What's more, the timing and the suspense are remarkable, making it impossible to tear yourself away from the drama.

But break away I did when I heard soft drumbeats coming from a temple in a walled compound a quarter mile away. Within those walls, old people were dancing awkwardly in the moonlight as they paid homage to the moon goddess. Some were so feeble that they had to be supported by companions. My first reaction on seeing them was to think it was grotesque. But before long I was saying to myself, "How beautiful..."

As dawn was breaking, the revelers dispersed. I made my way slowly back to my hotel along the shoreline. Rounding a bend I saw my four-room "hotel" and then its night watchman, who was running straight toward me. When he caught up with me he seized one of my wrists in terror, and trembling with fear he nearly swept me off my feet as he dragged me home.

I slept for a short spell and woke up in time for breakfast. Passing the front desk I asked the hotel manager what the ruckus had been about. He carefully explained to me that dawn is the time when ghosts roam the shoreline, and the poor watchman had been terrified at the prospect that one of them might possess me.

In that very moment I learned the true meaning of hospitality. The night watchman had risked his life to save the life of a stranger, a foreign scholar, who was simply trying to get home for the night.

CLOSER TO HOME

Not all sacred places on this planet lie outside America. In Death Valley shortly after midnight one night, I was awakened by a hoot owl or coyote — I was too sound asleep to discern which — that seemed to be calling me. Slipping on trousers and a jacket, I went out and for a half hour walked the lonesome road. Meditators try to empty their minds, and I think I came as close to emptying mine on that walk as I have ever come. It was the timeless peace that can come when one is alert but mental processes are at a standstill.

Another night I was taken to a night club by two students who had met in one of my classes, fallen in love, and married. The club was small, and we descended a few steps to enter it. An entertainer arrived with his guitar, sitting on a chair in front of a microphone. He looked gloomy and was probably depressed. Not once did he look anyone in the face. But I remember — and love — one of the songs he sang:

> I'm not the guy that's got the most.
> Of this here town I'm not the toast!
> Don't try to make me what I'm not.
> Just tryin' to get by with what I've got.

That song helps me down when I suspect that I am becoming infatuated with myself.

STURGIS, MICHIGAN

As exotic as our world travels were, I must agree with the Vietnamese Buddhist monk Thich Nhat Hanh, who says that the real value of pilgrimages of the sort we were on is that they help us see, upon our return, that our own backyards are also sacred ground.

In that light I will close this chapter about what I fondly call my love affair with the world by relating two anecdotes from the pleasant but otherwise nondescript town of Sturgis, Michigan. They were told to me by my aunt and uncle, who lived there, and I have never forgotten them.

In their day, in the years just after the Depression, Sturgis was not much more than a cluster of neighborhoods, each of which featured a cobbler and a barber. One day my aunt took one of her sandals to the cobbler and asked him to stitch the strap that had fallen off. The cobbler turned out to be Amish, and when she returned to his shop to pick up her sandal, the strap had been securely sewn back on. But to her everlasting surprise and delight he had also, at his own discretion and without expecting any recompense, neatly patched a hole in the toe of the sandal.

Now for my uncle. In his day, barbershops always offered the services of a bootblack, who would polish your shoes while your hair was being cut. My uncle was waiting for his turn in the barber's chair when the preceding customer climbed down out of it, and with an exaggerated wink at my uncle, handed the bootblack a fifty-dollar bill.

Whether he was intending to show off his wealth or to embarrass the poor bootblack, we will never know.

Nevertheless, the bootblack was unperturbed. He simply placed the bill carefully in his breast pocket. Then, reaching into his hip pocket, he extracted from it a wad of bills from which he peeled off forty-nine one-dollar bills. Then he pulled three quarters from his side pocket and thanked his patron, the owner of the barbershop, and handed the bills and the coins to the astonished customer.

It so happened that this was the last day of the month. The bootblack was in clover because he was planning to go to the bank during his lunch break to deposit his entire month's earnings.

When my uncle told me this story he said, "Huston, you should have seen the expression on that customer's face!"

Chapter Eight

Being Detained and Interrogated in the World's Largest Police Station

I n 1969–1970 I was one of three professors who conducted thirty students in an academic year around the world to study cultures on location. Four of these students were from Syracuse, where I was a professor at the time — Raymond Garauon, Kenneth Sky, Kenneth Gilbert, and Kim Smith — and the other twenty-six were from twenty-six other universities.

The theme for the year was "The Quest for Utopia." The political scientist on our faculty had us study political parties and communism, which promised the utopia of a classless society. A stop in the Soviet Union had been scheduled, as well as one in Sweden (the most advanced socialist country) and one in England, to study its form of parliamentary democracy. Our anthropology professor lodged us in utopian communes in Japan, and I lodged us in ashrams in India.

I recall a very successful commune in Japan that made thick tatami mats to sleep on. At the veritable feast of a supper they mounted for us there was a dispenser of hot saki, in which I'm afraid we all overindulged.

It was at the height of the Cold War (with its rallying cry of "Workers of the world, unite!"), when there were communist parties in every country of the world. So our political science professor arranged for us to anticipate our stop in the Soviet Union by visiting the headquarters of the Communist Party in Tokyo and hearing a lecture by its chairman. That went well. All our students were wearing red ties, and they decided to prolong this brush with communism. One of these students spoke a little Russian, and he had found the address of a small Russian tearoom. The students planned to go there and then afterward have dinner at the one Russian restaurant in Tokyo. Everyone was in high spirits — the day was turning into a lark.

However, there turned out to be a fly in the ointment. Japan was alert to the danger of a Communist takeover. Every day there were large parades of people waving red flags and shouting slogans, and plainclothes secret-service men were everywhere. They were monitoring our little group, and this Russian-themed day looked suspicious to them.

So, as we waited for the bus that would take us to the tearoom, a well-dressed gentleman approached me and, showing me his police badge, told me to tell our group that I would not be joining them for tea and dinner and would meet up with them at their hotel. His chauffeur was waiting for him, and the car delivered us to the Shinjuku Police Station, which is the largest police station in the world. Another agent was waiting for us at the door.

Slowly, the agent escorted me to the elevator, and when we exited on the second floor we came into a huge room filled with young men who were poring over pages of photographs and identifying the students we had been photographing in Communist Party parades. We were on the espionage floor of the station.

My escort took me to a small private room in which there were two chairs on opposite sides of a table. He closed the door and explained in broken English that he would be asking me some questions and writing down my answers. Courteously, he explained that at the close of his interview he would read to me what he had written so I could enter any corrections that might be needed.

The agent began with the usual questions: name, home address, age, next of kin, citizenship, profession, references, and the like. Gradually, he moved on to what most interested him. What was my income? To what political party did I belong? Did I have a bank account? Any savings? Property? Had I ever been arrested? Imprisoned? Had I received any honors or awards?

By this time my dander was rising.

This inquisition was an insult, I thought to myself. I wanted to be having dinner with my wife and our group.

When the question about honors and awards came I let him have it. I began by rattling off the number of books I had written, the awards I had received, and the eight honorary degrees that had been conferred on me.

When my interrogator had completed his questions and was reading his report back to me I found that eight times I had been designated a "national treasure." With that honorific I was released from custody and given a private car and driver to take me back to our hotel.

The next morning Kendra and I found a beautiful coffee-table book of Japanese art waiting for us at our hotel desk.

THE TRADITION OF HONORIFICS

In traditional Japan days would culminate with the *O furo*, *O* being an honorific, like "noble," and *furo* being "bath." The shape of the bathtub was such that one could only squat down in it in the fetal position, and one washed, soaped, and rinsed oneself before climbing into the tub. The entire family, beginning with the eldest, would bathe in the tub, which was heated by a fire below, and firewood was always scarce in Japan. Children were admonished not to leave the bathwater dirty, and that admonition moved into our family as a way of saying, "Clean up after yourself," "Don't leave dirty dishes in the sink," and so on.

Now, Japan has some two hundred temple gardens that are among the most beautiful in the world. The most famous of these is Ryoanji, in Kyoto. This magnificent garden houses a stone basin behind a tiny tea-ceremony hut, and the basin has a square indentation into which water flows from a nearby spring through a split bamboo pole with its notches removed.

There are Japanese characters on the basin, elevated in bas-relief, and I find them most interesting. Originally this indentation was a circle, but to fit better into other parts of characters it has been transformed into a square. When the square, enlarged to form a basin, appears at the bottom of a character, it is an archaic rendering of the pronoun I. When it appears on the right-hand side of the basin, the word is *know*. On the left-hand side the word is *only*, and at the bottom the word is *plenty*. So, from the bamboo dipper that is on top of the stone basin one can take a sip of water and "know only plenty."

I fell in love with that basin.

One day I saw a replica of it in a stone store and told Kendra that I didn't care if it meant mortgaging our house; I wanted that basin in our backyard. Of course, transporting it back to America took some doing. The basin probably weighed a literal ton. Nevertheless, we contracted with an export shipper and a railway express company in the States to have it shipped home.

Eventually, a delivery truck turned up in our driveway, in

Syracuse. The driver slid the crate holding the stone basin down a plank at the back of his truck, and left it there in our driveway. Then he dismissively handed me his clipboard with the contract on it, and said, "I'm not responsible for getting that crate where you want it."

Undeterred, I signed the paper and he drove off. Fortunately, it was possible to turn the basin on its side and roll it to a corner of our backyard.

When Kendra and I moved to Berkeley, we brought the basin with us. To this day, it sits in a corner of the backyard of our first Berkeley house, on Avenida Road, on the crest of the hills overlooking San Francisco Bay.

Recently, I decided to write to the San Francisco Zen Center and offer to give the basin to them for their meditation garden.

Chapter Nine

Magic and Mystery
on the Roof of the World

At three in the morning, on a full-moon night in October 1969, high in the foothills of the Himalayan mountains, there fell on my ears the holiest sound I have ever heard. Here is the story.

Debarred from Tibet because it was not then open to American citizens, I was on my way to research Tibetan Buddhism in a refugee monastery in North India. Actually, even if I could have entered Tibet I could not have found what I was looking for, for the Chinese had emptied the monasteries and put their monks to work building roads in the high mountains.

The train labored slowly up the mountain on which the monastery I was seeking was perched, but the railway tracks ended at Dalhousie, which is now in Pakistan. From there I climbed a steep path for about half a mile, and when I heard the sound of chanting I knew I was nearing my destination. When I reached the monastery's entrance I was ushered to the abbot's small bungalow. A large bowl of hot Tibetan tea was placed in my hands.

I have traveled a great deal and have encountered only two foods I have disliked. One was *poi* in Hawaii, which I imagine is what wallpaper paste tastes like, and the other is the Tibetan yak butter tea, a large bowl of which I was holding in my hands. I was desperately thirsty from my long climb up the mountain and took a big gulp from the bowl before the taste registered on me with a shock. Swallowing the tea brought to mind the prayer that a woman missionary to Africa said she prayed when at her welcoming banquet she was served monkey soup, a local delicacy that was made by throwing a live monkey into a pot of boiling water.

"Lord, I'll put it down," she prayed, "and you keep it down."

This recollection applied perfectly to my predicament. I could just see myself throwing up all over the beautiful Tibetan carpets that were laid across the floor before me.

Later, I learned how traditional Tibetan tea was made. You begin with a four-foot-long piece of bamboo, the notches of which have been excised. Throw into it a large dollop of rancid yak butter, followed by a handful of rock salt. That salt is all to the good, for it cuts the grease of the yak butter. Still, it doesn't keep the result from tasting, well, foul. I think you could comb the dictionary and not find a better descriptive word for the taste of that authentic tea: *foul*.

Fortunately, after submitting to that protocol bowl of welcoming tea, I descended to the ranks of commoners, who drank Indian tea.

As luck would have it, I had arrived on the evening of the highest holy day of the Tibetan year. So we all retired early because the four-day *puja*, or religious ceremony, was to begin at 3:00 a.m. the next morning.

Shortly before the designated hour, I heard shuffling footsteps on the trails and, after a brief ablution, I was told, "We have no special bathroom." That translates into God's great outdoors being their bathroom. I followed the monks to the large ceremonial tent, which was standing in for the monastery building that was being built for the Tibetan refugees. The eighty-eight monks, which was a mere one-tenth of the number in their original home at the Portola Palace, in Lhasa, were seated on six rows of thin mats, three rows facing each other on the aisle that led to the altar. I was directed to a pad at the end of one of those rows.

Promptly at 3:00 a.m. the chanting began. For the first forty minutes it was a deep guttural monotone — rhythmic in its seven syllables that were endlessly repeated but tonally unvarying. Echoing out of centuries of unquestioned belief, it was impressive in a way, but it was monotonous.

It was still dark outside. The naked 25-watt lightbulb that hung in the middle of the tent seemed only to intensify the gloom. I was tired from my travels. What I am leading up to is that I dozed off — only to be jolted into wakefulness by an uncanny sound.

What had been a numbing, monotonous monotone had splayed into a beautiful tonic chord — a first, a third, and a fifth. It felt as if I was suddenly surrounded by an angelic choir. My first thought was that I must be dreaming. But when I opened my eyes I saw the rows of monks and remembered where I was.

Though the chanting was beautiful, I found it puzzling. This harmonic chord was something I thought I understood as a Western invention, in contrast to Asian music, which relies on rhythm and melodic line.

But *that* puzzle was nothing compared to what followed.

Suddenly the choir cut out, leaving it all to a cantor. And there he was, singing the three-toned chord all by himself! To put it more accurately, the cantor was singing a solo chord.

For the rest of the four-day *puja*, the monks' chanting alternated between the guttural monotone, the chord sung by the choir, and the cantor singing the solo chord.

The four days gave me plenty of time to think. Curiously, my first thought was that my colleague Klaus Liepman, then the music director at MIT, where I taught at the time, would never believe me. I knew I had to find a way to present him with unassailable proof. Then I had a brainstorm. The day after the *puja* ended I excused myself and went to the local high school, where I found a small German tape recorder. I borrowed it and took it to the monastery, where the monks were kind enough to oblige with my request to repeat their performance so I might have what I needed.

When I returned to MIT, I asked around about who was working on the acoustics of the human voice. My inquiries led me to a part of the campus I had not been to before, and the laboratory of Professor Kenneth Stevens. When I reached the designated room I found a Please Enter sign posted on the door. When I did as told, I was greeted with "How are you?" in hugely exaggerated inflections that dipped and peaked as the professor's computer cordially welcomed me into his laboratory!

Startled but amused, I soon learned that Stevens was working on creating a device that would translate spoken words into writing. Now perfected, the device was then at the rudimentary stage, and later in our conversation Professor Stevens played me an early-stage example of his invention. The professor spoke into the device, and the resulting printout of his spoken words, "Time flies like an arrow," came out as, "A certain species of flies likes to eat arrows."

Now back to business.

When I entered the room Stevens stood up from his desk and greeted me. I held out my hand with the small cassette tape in my palm and explained what I had on it. *This was fun*, I thought, knowing I had discovered something new to his brilliantly trained ears, a sound he would be interested in because no one outside those monasteries had ever heard it before. But as I described my encounter with the Tibetan monks I detected the faint trace of a smile crossing his face, as if he was eagerly waiting to straighten out this philosophy professor on his so-called explanation.

Then I played the tape I had made in India of the chanting monks. When he heard their otherworldly chanting the expression on his face changed dramatically.

"This is a sound," he said, "the Western world has never heard before."

That exchange led to a friendship that eventuated in the introduction of a new term in the lexicography of musicology: *multiphonic chanting*. The chanting also led to an article in the *Journal of the American Acoustical Society*, which Professor Stevens co-authored with me.

My encounter with multiphonic chanting is the sole empirical discovery of my career. It did my ego no end of good, and, moreover, it also raised my profile at MIT, because it is the job of MIT professors to discover things, while we philosophers merely sit around and ruminate.

I had had my moment in the sun. I had experienced the rush of exaltation that comes from making an empirical discovery.

MEETING HIS HOLINESS

My time at the refugee monastery led to one other life-altering encounter. Shortly after my arrival, one the several monks there who was learning English asked me if I had paid respects to His Holiness the Dalai Lama, in Dharamsala, India.

"I hadn't planned to visit him," I said, honestly. "He has the burdens of his people on his shoulders. I do not want to add to those burdens."

"What?" the monk exclaimed. Then, almost shouting, he said, "You came halfway around the world to study our tradition, and you are going to bypass the man who incarnates, no, who is the essence of our tradition?"

When it was put that way I realized I wanted very much to meet His Holiness. Relieved, the monk scheduled an appointment for me.

Thus emboldened, I traveled by bus to Dharamsala. Upon arrival I was directed to the bungalow where His Holiness was living.

Our encounter brought a great surprise.

Standing on the threshold of the bungalow, I showed my calling card to his sentry and was waved in. As I rounded the corner of the bungalow's veranda, His Holiness approached me from its other end with a warm smile. We shook hands, and I was immediately struck by the firmness of his grip. His handshake wasn't the bone-crunching grip of a Texas rancher, but one whose firmness still made my hand feel like a limp fish because his spiritual strength was coming through.

His Holiness ushered me into his small living room, and we seated ourselves. I had told myself in advance not to stay more than ten minutes, because I was well aware of the tremendous burden on his shoulders and was grateful to him for the graciousness he had shown by receiving me at all.

After what I believed was my ten minutes of *darshan*, I thanked him for receiving me and, wishing him the very best for his people, stood up to go. He too arose but paused for a moment before shaking hands. Although his English was rudimentary then, and he conversed mostly through an interpreter, I heard him say softly to himself, "I must decide what is important."

Then, with that wonderful smile and an accompanying hand gesture he said, "Please be seated."

When I next stood up, an hour and forty minutes had elapsed of the most astonishing morning of my life.

What won me this gift turned out to be an unintended ruse, an accidental deception. The Dalai Lama's lifelong interest in science and technology is well-known. But that day I had no idea of his avid curiosity about Western science. As a boy he loved to take watches and telescopes apart to see how they worked. Since my calling card carried the words Massachusetts Institute of Technology in its lower left-hand corner, he thought he had a real live scientist in his living room, and he was determined not to squander the opportunity.

Specifically, the spiritual leader of the Tibetan people wanted to know, first, what I could tell him about the big bang. He had heard the phrase, but that was all. Coincidentally, a month before I left home I had heard a lecture by Harlow Shapley, the astrophysicist at Harvard, who said that evidence was mounting that the universe expands and contracts like an accordion.

"According to Professor Shapley," I informed His Holiness, "the *bang bang bang* would be a better epithet."

His Holiness acknowledged that the astrophysicist was right, which made me immediately look forward to telling Shapley on my return of the support he had gained from a holy man with a brilliant mind on the other side of the globe.

The other topic on the Dalai Lama's mind was DNA. He had heard a little about it and said he needed to know if it had any bearing on reincarnation, a topic in which we might say he has a certain vested interest. This took longer, but he concluded that it had no such bearing.

That morning won me the lifelong friendship of the man, who in a sense has acted as a therapist to those suffering in the world. In his book *The Universe in a Single Atom: The Convergence of Science and Spirituality*, he writes: "When I count my teachers of

99

science, I include Huston Smith among them, although I am not sure whether he would himself approve of this."

THE DALAI LAMA COMES TO AMERICA

When I returned to America, I visited the State Department's Immigration Office and helped to secure a three-week visa for the Dalai Lama to visit the United States, a visit I monitored. His simple request for the tour was that it include three stops: the Harvard Divinity School, where he hoped to deepen his understanding of Christianity; Syracuse University, where I was then teaching; and the University of California at Berkeley, because the state has the most Asian immigrants of any state in America.

His Syracuse visit included an evening lecture and a symposium the following afternoon. The only thing I remember about the evening lecture was that during the question period someone in the audience asked what he should do with his anger. The Dalai Lama was still speaking through an interpreter, but he understood the question and sang out, "Control it!"

At the symposium, one of the attendees goaded the Dalai Lama, trying to get him to assert that Buddhism is superior to Christianity. His Holiness heard him out and then said, "If I say anything against the Lord Jesus, the Buddha would scold me."

One other memory stands out from that afternoon. The symposium was invitational, but word had gotten around, and the hallway leading to the conference room was packed. A local Japanese Zen monk had been waiting the longest and was at the head of the line. When the Dalai Lama appeared, the monk held out an infant in his arms, who he said was desperately sick. The Dalai Lama held the baby's cheeks in both hands and gazed into his eyes. He then touched his forehead to the baby's — the Tibetan mode of conferring a blessing — and held it there for more than a minute, touching foreheads being the Buddhist counterpart to Christianity's "laying on of hands." When he lifted his head and continued down the waiting line, I glanced at the monk whose baby the Dalai Lama had blessed. Tears were streaming down the monk's cheeks.

Years later, I was able to take my grandson, Anthony, to hear His Holiness at a conference in Oakland, California. During the invitation-only breakfast I was able to shake hands and say hello to my old friend, and asked him if he would grant my grandson the same honor of touching his forehead to that of my grandson. Graciously, he agreed. At that moment I believed I had given Anthony the greatest gift possible, a blessing for the rest of his life.

HEALING THE HEALER

It stands to reason that the Dalai Lama should have his own physicians, and it happens that many years ago, by standing in a long line in Oakland, Kendra and I were treated by one of them.

However, that visit was rather perfunctory. It was a visit to diagnose, not to treat. The doctor felt our pulses, said that we were in good health, and gave us some herbs. We left the physician and went on our way.

Years later, however, we came across an account about the healing powers of Tibetan medicine written by a Western doctor, Richard Selzer, who had had the opportunity of observing the then physician to the Dalai Lama treat a patient. The account here is drawn from Selzer's book *Mortal Lessons: Notes on the Art of Surgery* and is unusually long for an extract. But I have decided to include it, both for the way it honors the Tibetans at this time when they are facing the prospect of genocide, and also because I find it inspiring and suspect that readers of this book will also find it moving. Here is Selzer's account, included here with his kind permission:

> On the bulletin board in the front hall of the hospital where I work, there appeared an announcement. "Yeshi Dhonden,"

it read, "will make rounds at six o'clock on the morning of June 10." The particulars were then given, followed by a notation: "Yeshi Dhonden is Personal Physician to the Dalai Lama." I am not so leathery a skeptic that I would knowingly ignore an emissary from the gods... Thus, on the morning of June 10, I join the clutch of whitecoats waiting in the small conference room adjacent to the ward selected for the rounds. The air in the room is heavy with ill-concealed dubiety and suspicion of bamboozlement. At precisely six o'clock, he materializes, a short, golden, barrelly man dressed in a sleeveless robe of saffron and maroon. His scalp is shaven, and the only visible hair is a scanty black line above each hooded eye.

He bows in greeting while his young interpreter makes the introduction. Yeshi Dhonden, we are told, will examine a patient... [whose] diagnosis is unknown to [him] as it is to us... We are further informed that for the past two hours Yeshi Dhonden has purified himself by bathing, fasting, and prayer. I, having breakfasted well, performed only the most desultory of ablutions, and given no thought at all to my soul, glance furtively at my fellows. Suddenly, we seem a soiled, uncouth lot.

The patient had been awakened early and told that she was to be examined by a foreign doctor... so when we enter her room, the woman shows no surprise. She has long ago taken on that mixture of compliance and resignation that is the facies of chronic illness. This was to be but another in an endless series of tests and examinations. Yeshi Dhonden steps to the bedside while the rest stand apart, watching. For a long time he gazes at the woman, favoring no part of her body with his eyes, but seeming to fix his glance at a place just above her supine form. I, too, study her. No physical sign nor obvious symptom gives a clue to the nature of her disease.

At last he takes her hand, raising it in both of his own. Now he bends over the bed in a kind of crouching stance, his head drawn down into the collar of his robe. His eyes are closed as he feels for her pulse. In a moment he has found the spot, and for the next half hour he remains thus, suspended above the patient like some exotic golden bird with folded wings, holding the pulse of the woman beneath his fingers, cradling her hand in his. All the power of the man seems to have been drawn down into this one purpose. It is palpation of the pulse raised to the state of ritual. From the foot of the bed where I stand, it is as though he and the patient have entered a special place of isolation, or apartness, above which a vacancy hovers, and across which no violation is possible. After a moment, the woman rests back upon her pillow. From time to time, she raises her head to look at the strange figure above her, then sinks back once more. I cannot see their hands joined in a correspondence that is exclusive, intimate, his fingertips receiving the voice of her sick body through the rhythm and throb she offers at her wrist. All at once I am envious — not of him, not of Yeshi Dhonden for his gift of beauty and holiness, but of her. I want to be held like that, touched so, *received*. And I know that I, who have palpated a hundred thousand pulses, have not felt a single one.

At last Yeshi Dhonden straightens, gently places the woman's hand upon the bed, and steps back.... All this while he has not uttered a single word. As he nears the door, the woman raises her head and calls out to him in a voice at once urgent and serene. "Thank you, doctor," she says, and touches with her other hand the place he had held on her wrist, as though to recapture something that he had visited there. Yeshi Dhonden turns back for a moment to gaze at her, then steps into the corridor. Rounds are at an end.

We are seated once more in the conference room. Yeshi

Dhonden speaks for the first time, in soft Tibetan sounds that I have never heard before. He has barely begun when the young interpreter begins to translate, the two voices continuing in tandem — a bilingual fugue, the one chasing the other. It is like the chanting of monks. He speaks of winds coursing through the body of the woman, currents that break against barriers, eddying. These vortices are in her blood, he says. The last spendings of an imperfect heart. Between the chambers of her heart, long, long before she was born, a wind had come and blown open a deep gate that must never be opened. Through it charge the full waters of her river, as the mountain stream cascades in the springtime, battering, knocking loose the land, and flooding her breath. Thus he speaks, and is silent.

"May we now have the diagnosis?" a professor asks.

The host of these rounds, the man who knows, answers.

"Congenital heart disease," he says. "Interventricular septal defect, with resultant heart failure."

A gateway in the heart, I think. That must not be opened. Through it charge the full waters that flood her breath. So! Here then is the doctor listening to the sounds of the body to which the rest of us are deaf. He is more than doctor. He is priest.... Then a jubilation possesses me, and I feel myself touched by something divine.

As it does me as well, simply by reading Dr. Selzer's beautifully written account.

THE TIBETANS
AND THE GRATEFUL DEAD

Mickey Hart, a drummer for the erstwhile Grateful Dead, is also a serious ethnomusicologist who now works with the Smithsonian

Institution. Fascinated by the Tibetan monks' multiphonic chanting, he put the infrastructure of the Dead to work and helped organize six sellout coast-to-coast tours with twelve of the Gyuto monks.

One evening the monks were returning to Mickey's ranch, in Northern California, after a performance in the University of California's Zellerbach Auditorium, in Berkeley. When the van reached the Marin side of the Richmond Bridge, out of the blue the monks asked the driver to pull over to the side of the road. They told Mickey that they sensed evil in the vicinity, and they wanted to alleviate it. Little did they know that at that moment they were passing San Quentin, a maximum-security penitentiary. Visibly moved, they asked if they could go into the prison and bless the inmates.

Mickey was skeptical, but he asked the sentry on duty, who referred the matter to his superior. The monks were admitted to the entrance, which was separated from the prison proper by about twelve yards. On the opposite side was an electric fence featuring elevated cages, which housed sharpshooters with cocked rifles.

The prison chaplain told us about a Christian group of prisoners who met regularly to pray and sing hymns. They were summoned, and for about half an hour they alternated with the monks, one group singing and praying, and the other group chanting. The monks were so moved by their encounter with the prisoners that they returned several times to repeat the ritual.

Later, I accompanied Mickey to the San Francisco Airport to say farewell to the monks, who where returning to India, for their final tour had ended. As the stairs for boarding the plane descended to the runway, the monks regrouped themselves and chanted a farewell blessing on the land that they were leaving. The passengers in the corridor who were proceeding to their departure gates were so captivated they stopped and clustered around the monks, listening intently. As the last monk disappeared into the plane and the door was closing, a woman asked us in wide-eyed wonder, "What was *that* all about?"

As if to answer her emphatically, Mickey shouted out to the departing monks the famous line from *Star Wars*, "May the Force be with you!"

Then, turning to me, Mickey said, "What am I saying? May the Force be with *me*! They already have it!"

WHAT WE HAVE IN COMMON

Mickey's fascination with the monks' ethereal multiphonic chanting, which I had helped bring to the attention of the world, inspired him to reserve huge halls to bring their music to the attention of the "Deadheads," Grateful Dead fans, as well as those interested in Tibetan culture. Attracting overflow crowds to vast auditoriums was only one way he figured out to persuade the public why they should go to a concert held by Tibetan monks.

His other strategy was to play the monks' music on the radio. Being with the Grateful Dead made it possible for him to get booked onto any talk show in the country. So before the first concert he procured an interview on KQED's *Forum*, one of the most listened-to and respected shows. And he dragged me along as the person who had discovered multiphonic chanting.

The interview went well, and when it came time for the wrap-up, the host said, "Our time is nearly up, but I have one more question for you, Mickey. I'm going to give it to you right between the eyes. Huston Smith here is no problem; he teaches this stuff. But what is a member of the Grateful Dead doing with Tibetan monks?"

Without hesitation, Mickey replied, "We're both in the *transportation business*."

Chapter Ten

Lions on the Serengeti Plain

A t Olduvai Gorge, in South Africa, I was told that if I walked two miles from my broken-down car to the nearest highway at twilight, "You *must* be eaten by lions."

Those words sounded to me like a command. They came toward the close of the day in which I *would* have been eaten by lions on the Serengeti Plain, had I not been rescued by twelve robust Masai warriors.

Here is the story.

To attend a conference at a school in the late 1960s, I had flown to Dar es Salaam, the Haven of Peace, the commerce capital of Tanzania. The city abuts the Serengeti Plain. Anticipating an adventure, encountering big game in their natural habitat, I did a bit of research. I learned that this plain is the sanctuary of the Masai tribe and that it harbors more wild game than any comparable stretch of territory in all of East Africa. The plain may seem empty, but actually it swarms with as much life as the waters of tropical seas do. It is webbed with the paths of wildebeests and gazelles, and its hollows and valleys are trampled by thousands of zebras. Buffalo invade the pastures, and occasionally the droll shape of a rhinoceros can be seen plodding across the horizon like a boulder that has come to life and is stalking its own form of adventure.

Learning this, I knew I couldn't leave the country without a glimpse of some of these animals. There were no tours in those days, but I found a fly-by-night rental car agency that had a rickety Renault that was so far gone they were desperate to get it off their lot. They sold it to me for the price of a rental.

So, as the sudden owner of a Tanzanian car, really a jalopy, I set out for the Serengeti. There were no road maps in the car, which figured, because there were no roads. Eventually, I did encounter one road sign, which I couldn't read, and in any case it had fallen over, which meant I couldn't even tell which way its arrows were meant to point.

As far as the eye could see, there was nothing but grass, rocks, and a few animals and trees.

If that wasn't ominous enough, I was scarcely into the plain when I had a flat tire and was forced to get out of the car to change it, which was not the safest or sanest thing to do in that part of the world. While I was busy cranking the car up with the tire jack, a curious giraffe ambled over and leaned across my shoulder. A little farther into the desert the car's motor sputtered and with a little gasp gave up the ghost.

When we rent a car in America we assume the tank will be full. Not in Tanzania. They give you about enough to get you out of the lot, but I didn't know that and hadn't checked. The gas gauge registered full when I left, but it didn't work. When I checked it later at Olduvai Gorge the tank turned out to be empty.

So there I was, with my car totally stalled and unable to think of what to do next. The car was as hot as an oven, so I couldn't stay in it — but it was dangerous to leave it.

I knew that big cats sleep during the midday sun and prowl in the cool of the evening, but fortunately, there were no lions in sight. To make matters even more dramatic, I could see dry animal bones scattered around the car — ominous portents of the fate that awaited me.

I ate my packed lunch, started rationing my last bottle of water, and tried to think of a plan of action. None suggested itself.

Then two tall figures seemed to appear on the horizon. I say "seemed to appear" because in the sunlight that was shimmering from the heat I thought they might be mirages. I looked again and they seemed to move, so I started toward them. But with every step I took they retreated. I quickened my pace, making frantic gestures of distress, and they gradually slowed their pace and allowed me to catch up with them.

They turned out to be two Masai warriors, disconcertingly tall, who wore nothing but spears taller than themselves and strips of flapping cloth that covered their shoulders and did their best to ward off the scorching sun.

What was I to do? I was in human company but without words to communicate. *Something* had to be done! I seized one of them by the wrist and marched him back to my dysfunctional car, with his companion in tow. This seemed to amuse them, and why wouldn't it? What did my pile of junk have to do with *them*?

The two of them conversed, but then they started to leave, a prospect that terrified me. I seized one of my hostage's wrists to stall him. He and his friend were my only lifeline, and I couldn't allow it to be severed. They laughed and talked, and then one of them turned away and began running off toward the distant horizon in that beautiful, long, noble stride of the Masai runners, leaving his hostage with me.

When the first runner returned a little later he had a small boy in tow, who knew a few words of English, namely, *hello* and *good-bye*. Someone must have taught him those words. Hoping that he might understand me I pointed in several different directions, and asked plaintively, "School, school. Where? Where?" The boy gave little sign of comprehension, and my hopes waned. But after conversing with his companions a little more, he and the man who had fetched him went off together, leaving me once again with my hostage.

About an hour later, they returned with ten adult cohorts. As the sun set that evening, one of the most bizarre scenes that had ever unfolded on the Serengeti Plain took place. A team of Masai warriors were pushing a dilapidated Renault across on the trackless Serengeti Plain with a lost American scholar sitting comfortably at the wheel. My human propellers were pushing me out of danger, turning the experience into a great lark, chattering and laughing at the same time and sounding like a flock of happy birds.

My first thought was, *"Who is listening?"* This was followed immediately by, *"Who cares?"* because my newfound friends were having such a good time helping me.

Six miles across the plain they pushed me in the old Renault, finally delivering me to the putative "school," which the boy had actually understood in some way. It turned out to be a building at Olduvai Gorge, where a decade earlier Louis and Mary Leakey, along with their son Richard, had discovered the tooth that the press heralded as the discovery that "set the human race back a million years."

OLDUVAI GORGE

In those days the Leakeys divided their year. For six months they excavated, and for the balance of the year they left the excavating to a crew of workmen headed by an overseer who could speak English, while they oversaw the Museum of Natural History in Nairobi.

When I arrived at the gorge the first thing I told my host was that I wanted to pay the Masai handsomely for saving my life but knew of course that my traveler's checks would be useless to them.

"So, please, will you reward them?" I suggested. "I will repay you." I never saw what my host actually presented them with, but the warriors wandered off chirping like happy birds.

Then I told the overseer my story. When he asked me what I proposed to do, I asked him how far we were from the highway, and when he said two miles I said I would walk there and hitch a ride to the city. The next day, I promised him, I would return with a tow truck that could transport the car back to the rental agency in Dar es Salaam. It was then that he spoke the words recounted above: "If you walk the highway at this time of day, you *must* be eaten by lions."

I decided to wait until morning.

At supper I slaked my thirst. I was ushered to the simple bungalow that the Leakeys lived in while they worked on-site. That incredible day ended with me sleeping on Louis Leakey's cot, drinking the whiskey on the floor beside it, and cursing the two of them for their inhospitality in not being present to welcome me in person.

Incidentally, the press credited Louis with discovering the infamous tooth, but actually it was Mary who had discovered it. I sent that correction to *Ms. Magazine*, but they didn't print it.

That encounter on the Serengeti left me with a profound sense

of human connectedness. There we were, as different in every way
— ethnically, linguistically, and culturally — as any two groups
on our planet. Yet without a single word in common, we had connected. They understood my predicament and responded with a
will and — just as important — with style.

That adventure taught me to beware of the differences that
blind us to the unity that binds us.

Chapter Eleven

Be Ever at the Ready as You Ramble

"**W**hen you go hunting, be ever at the ready as you ramble," a Native American friend once told me. "Hold your shotgun in both hands (not by your side as if it were an old-fashioned suitcase), or the quail is likely to take off from the underbrush before you can get your gun to your shoulder."

My version of this wise advice, to be ever ready as I ramble, is to be alert to opportunities that present themselves. I will content myself with three examples of this kind of readiness.

The first took place in 1945, in San Francisco, when the United Nations was founded. At that time, to be *ever at the ready* meant crossing the Bay Bridge at five o'clock in the morning so I could squeeze my way into the huge auditorium in the San Francisco Opera House that had been adapted for the occasion.

What I recall most is the long debate as to the shape of the table where delegates from the UN would sit to discuss ongoing international problems. It was finally decided that the table should be *round* so that there would be no head at the table.

Some years later, Kendra and I purchased a wooden toolbox at a garage sale. It had seen better days, but the owner told us it had been used by the carpenter who constructed the elegant round table for the United Nations. Thus inspired by the coincidence, we bought it and used it until it disintegrated to the point where it was useless.

TRAVELS IN HAITI

A second example of being ever at the ready occurred during my years of teaching at Syracuse, between 1973 and 1983. Everyone at the university in those days headed south during spring break, and Kendra and I usually joined the throng.

One April, we went to Haiti with a friend who knew the wife of the cultural attaché there. The wife greeted us cordially and asked if we would like to accompany her to the weekly voodoo ceremony that she would be attending that evening, adding that it had become her "spiritual home" for the duration of her stay. This surprised us because we had gone along with the conventional view that voodoo was only the superstitious belief of the backward people who stuck pins into dolls for the purposes of hexing their enemies.

Being ever ready to ramble, we agreed to the unusual offer and accompanied the woman on a forty-five-minute drive that brought us to a clearing in the remote woodlands. When we arrived people were assembling, and we were quickly greeted by a tall, handsome man with an imposing bearing who wore a white suit and polished black shoes. Our host told us that he had studied at the Harvard Business School but had chosen to return to his homeland and was the leader of the group that was gathering as we spoke.

Drums began to beat. A bonfire was lit. A rooster was sacrificed on it. The leader pronounced a supplication for the healing of a sick person in one of the attending families. Then while Kendra and I watched from the sidelines the rest of the group began to dance in wild, abandoned free-form dancing, which our host avidly took part in.

One woman, who had been ill, suddenly stood up and began to dance. At first her dancing was graceful but it soon turned jerky, bizarre, even ecstatically erratic — so much so that the others had to protect her from her own flailing around so she didn't fall into the bonfire. One of the "lesser spirits," as the word *voodoo* suggests, had chosen her for its evening visitation. With the calming help of her family and friends, the woman slowly returned from her spirit trance and back to her normal senses, and the strange ceremony drew to a close.

On the drive back to our hotel we asked our host if what we thought had just transpired had actually happened.

"Was that flailing woman *possessed?*" Kendra asked.

"Yes, she was visited by the spirits," the woman said.

"What does it feel like when you are possessed?" I asked.

"She probably experienced nothing that she could actually describe or even remember," our host said. "A possession brings total amnesia."

But, she added, the sick patient we witnessed trance dancing had been healed through the ceremony.

TIANANMEN SQUARE

Now for my third example of *being ever at the ready*.

As is well-known, in 1989 Chinese students staged a demonstration in Tiananmen Square to protest the government's curtailment of civil liberties. And I was there.

After Mao Tse-tung died, China began to open up. The American Academy of Religion proposed to China's Bureau of Cultural

Affairs that it mount an International Symposium on Chinese Religions. The Chinese accepted the proposal. The United States offered to fund the symposium, and China offered to provide the venue.

At the agreed-upon date, after a long, exhausting flight, we Westerners arrived at the Beijing Airport at 1:00 a.m., to be greeted by rumors of unrest in the city. Nothing was clear, and we were exhausted, so we tumbled into our beds and slept. We were housed in double rooms, and my roommate was Ninian Smart, an Englishman who had been appointed chair of the Religious Studies Department at Santa Barbara, which may be (as of this writing), the best such department in the world. It just so happens that Ninian always carried a transistor radio with him to pick up the BBC news reports. When he turned on his radio at 6:00 a.m. the next morning the headline was that students had occupied Tiananmen Square to protest the censoring of the news and other curtailments of civil liberties.

Quickly we tumbled out of bed, awoke our confreres, went to the front desk, and ordered two taxis. Sick of Maoist repression, the city was elated by the uprising and people at the desk wrote "Foreign Visitors Support Student Demonstrations" in huge characters on stretches of computer paper and attached them to the sides of the taxis with strapping tape.

When we were within blocks of the square, the traffic jam of automobiles and buses and bicycles was being diverted by students with armbands, who were policing their own revolution. But because of the signs on our taxis we were waved into the very center of the square. The cheering students who packed the square greeted us enthusiastically and demanded a speech.

One of our number was a sinologist who was fluent in Chinese. When we singled him out, the students hoisted him to the top of the taxi. He delivered a short speech — "Democracy is not only for America. Democracy is not only for China. Democracy is for the whole world!" The student crowd's enthusiasm knew no bounds.

We left Beijing in high spirits, convinced that the student movement had advanced too far to be turned back, but we were tragically wrong. Tanks crushed the bodies of the first several rows of protesters, and the others fled.

The political persecution didn't end there. Sympathetic strikes had sprung up in all the major cities of China, and their leaders were being hunted down. Some managed to escape to America, and the Unitarian Church in Berkeley sheltered three or four of them. We hosted one of them for a week or so, and covered our tracks when anonymous phone calls asked for someone with a Chinese name. We could do this without lying because the Chinese students had adopted pseudonyms and we never learned their real names. To do so would have been too dangerous for them.

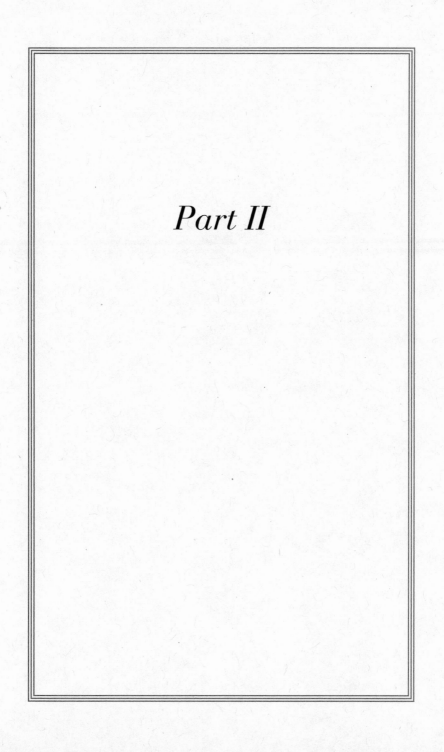

Part II

Chapter Twelve

Improbables

Nothing is too rum to be true.

— SAUL BELLOW, quoting a confirmed atheist wondering if he
would survive the death of his body on his deathbed

In 1982 I went back to China to visit Dzang Zok, the town where
I grew up. My return flight to America left from Shanghai, and
I scheduled my departure for a Monday so that I could attend
the Sunday service at the large bilingual church where our family
worshipped when we were in Shanghai. The church was packed
with an overflow crowd of congregants, many standing along the
walls, but I was offered a seat reserved for foreign visitors.

After the service I was taken to meet the retired pastor. When
I identified myself, his eyes filled with tears. "Your father taught
me English," he said, "and in thanks I would like to take you to
lunch."

As we were elbowing our way through the teeming throng of
people, my companion happened to glance up and, recognizing the

face of an old woman who was leaning over a third-floor balcony, he waved his arms and shouted, "Miss Yu, Miss Yu — look who I have here!"

She peered down, and after a few moments said, incredulously, "Could that be Huston?"

We went up to her apartment and sat in stunned silence for a few moments. Let me fill in the background here.

In 1919, the year I was born, sixty-three years before our serendipitous meeting, my parents had discovered that no education was provided for the girls in our town. So even before they built a church, my parents started a school for girls.

Yu Si-lei, Miss Yu to me, the woman sitting before me now, was its first principal. Later, she was sent to Scarritt College in Nashville, where she perfected her English and learned how to develop a curriculum for elementary schools. The Board of Missions then sent her back to found schools for girls all over China.

Improbably, we had bumped into each other because Miss Yu had not felt well enough that week to travel and visit her sister. She had postponed that visit for a week and so was at home at the propitious moment when we met her.

When we recovered from our shock at meeting again after five decades, we tried to fill in what had happened since we had last been together. Then in celebration we sang a hymn in Chinese to the accompaniment of her piano playing, and we prayed together. Greatly satisfied with our improbable encounter, the pastor and I departed for our delayed lunch.

ST. STEPHEN'S COLLEGE

During the semester that I taught at St. Stephen's College in Columbia, Missouri, I was taken to visit John Neihardt (1881–1973), poet laureate of Nebraska, who was then serving as a visiting professor of journalism at the University of Missouri. I looked forward to talking with him about his famous book, *Black Elk Speaks*, a beautiful and very influential portrayal of the Oglala Sioux prophet. But it turned out that he couldn't focus on our conversation about that book because of something that had happened the previous week.

The Neihardts had been involved in a minor car accident, and in those days insurance agents came to their clients' homes to determine what had happened. They were seated at the dining room table discussing the accident when the agent interrupted, saying, "Excuse me, but would you mind putting that dog out? He's making me nervous."

"What dog?" John asked.

"Oh, you know, that little black one," the agent said, glancing under the table. "Oh, he seems to have gone out by himself."

The Neihardts had *had* a black spaniel, to which they were as attached as if it had been their child, but he had died of old age the week before, and they were in deep mourning.

When the agent left, the Neihardts returned to the dining room table and sat together in stunned silence. Thereafter, John lost interest in completing his epic poem on Nebraska and founded the Center for the Study of Paranormal Phenomena, which still exists, and he willed his legacy, which included the significant income from *Black Elk Speaks*, to the center.

CHANNELING

When I joined the philosophy department at Washington University in 1948, its chairman, Charles Cory, was nearing retirement, and when I had won his confidence he introduced me to the strange phenomenon of *channeling*, a human being serving as a conduit for someone who for all practical purposes existed outside space and time.

My chairman said that night after night he had sat beside

Mrs. John Curran, who lived in the apartment directly across from his and who had transcribed a 640-page book that was published in 1917 as *The Sorry Tale: A Story of the Time of Christ*. Mrs. Curran said that she was receiving inner dictations from someone who said she was an Englishwoman living in the eighteenth century. In the 1800s, this would have been called mediumship. In biblical times it would have been called revelation. Kendra and I both believe that channeling — telepathy over time that spans varying lengths — happens. The channeled spirit identified herself as a woman with the marvelous name Patience Worth. She said that she was dictating the book to let the world know what happened on the day that Jesus died.

The improbables multiply.

The book came to Mrs. Curran in eighteenth-century English. Scholars have not found a single mistake in what she transcribed at breakneck speed, up to five thousand words a stretch without a single correction. She could stop in the middle of a paragraph and a day or week later begin again exactly where she had left off. And although it is impossible to check the facts that Patience Worth recounts, there is nothing in her book that does not accord with what historians know about the time and place of Jesus's life. It goes without saying that Mrs. Curran knew no more of first-century Palestine than a man in the street.

To indicate the profound reverence and power of what Patience Worth first called *A Sorry Tale*, but after a short pause said, "No. Change that to *The Sorry Tale*," I will quote a few lines from her poem about Jesus at the Sea of Galilee.

Calm eyes a-look 'cross sea.
The seething waters lap 'pon sands
At feet of Him. The day, a-bathed of blood,
A-soundeth 'mid the soothing of the sea's soft voice.
Earth, old, olden, yea,

And yet so youthed, so youthed!
And He a-sit, calm-eyed, years youthed,
And wisdom olded past the tell.

Patience Worth knew that her book would invite suspicion, but she was confident that it would carry the day: "Hark ye!... There shall be ones who shall tear at this cloth till it shreddeth, yet the shreds shall weave them back unto the whole 'pon love strands. For Love be the magic warp, and Love may ne'er die, but be born athin all hearts that sup the words."

A copy of *The Sorry Tale* is in my bookcase, but its usefulness is limited to documenting what I have written, for I find its two-hundred-year-old English unintelligible.

CHESTER CARLSON

Chester Carlson, inventor and physicist, invented a way to make dry photocopies — the most important discovery in printing since Gutenberg's printing press. I was invited to his house on the outskirts of Rochester, New York.

Chester had passed away, but his wife was interested in my books and used part of the patent money that came pouring in to build small reading rooms around the world that housed religious books, including mine. She invited me to their estate for a weekend, during which she told me this anecdote.

After supper each evening, she and Chester had a practice of withdrawing to their living room and meditating for half an hour. One evening Chester said, "We both believe that there is another world, but I am a scientist and I like proof. So let's meditate and ask that the other world prove its existence." A few minutes later they heard a loud bang that seemed to come from the ceiling, as if two clapboards had been slammed together. They glanced at each other and continued their meditation.

THE CLAIRVOYANT

Eileen Garrett, an Irish parapsychologist, was the most famous
clairvoyant Kendra and I have ever known. We had been introduced to her by a mutual friend, Arthur Young (designer of the
Bell helicopter), who had kindly filled us in about the background
of their relationship.

When Arthur was first introduced to Eileen she asked him if
he would hand her his pen, and after stroking it for a few moments
she proceeded to tell him things about himself that, as Arthur said,
she had no right or way to know.

The second time, Arthur took the initiative and sought her out
for her psychometric talent. In constructing a helicopter, it was
easy to figure out how to get it off the ground, but the trick was in
managing a safe landing. Once, when a helicopter had not landed
properly, Arthur took a piece of the rotator blade to Eileen. After
stroking it, Eileen told him that there was nothing wrong with the
vehicle, that it was a machine in good working order. The problem
was with its pilot, who she said was incompetent.

When Arthur looked deeper into the matter, he found that to
be exactly the case. Twice the pilot had tried to enter a monastery
but had been turned down on the grounds of mental instability.

Now for our part of the story. A congresswoman from Florida
had put her estate at Eileen's disposal while Congress was in session. One winter, Eileen invited our family to share the congresswoman's Florida mansion, replete with servants, for a week. I still
don't know what prompted the invitation. Perhaps she had read
some of my books, or perhaps she simply wanted company for the
week.

Be that as it may, the week was a happy one. She didn't use it
to brandish her talents, nor did we ask her to do so. It was simply
a week of warm companionship in a magnificent midwinter warm
and sunny setting, far from the frigid north.

A SUMMER IN MEXICO

In 1951 Kendra and I spent an interesting summer in Mexico. We spent most of our time in the beautiful town of San Miguel de Allende before it became a tourist attraction, but we also wanted to visit Mexico City, so we hired a car and a driver and headed off.

Mexico City is fascinating and beautiful, and we enjoyed ourselves immensely. Two days before we were scheduled to return to San Miguel, Kendra noticed a fabric in the window of a tailoring store that she thought would make a nice suit for me. We entered the store and explained that we would be leaving the city in two days.

"Would that allow enough time for you to make a suit?" I inquired. The tailor nodded and told us the price, then set to work taking my measurements, saying that we could return later that afternoon for a fitting.

Rejoicing that we had found just the right man for the job, we agreed to return later for the fitting, which we did, and then returned the next day to pick up the suit.

However, I was mortified when I pulled out my checkbook because the tailor shook his head and wagged his finger at us with great vigor.

"*¡Muy malo!*" he said. "Very bad!

We explained that we had clearly told him that we would be happy to pay by check.

Then, using probably the only two English words he knew, he said, "*Traveler's checks!*"

In other words, no personal checks.

We offered the pesos that we had, but the tailor wanted traveler's checks and we had just cashed our last ones.

We were at an impasse.

Frantically, I rifled through my wallet looking for something that would validate my credentials. I flashed a credit card, but that broke no ice. Suddenly something caught my eye, a revelation that requires an explanation.

At the time we were living in St. Louis, which is a baseball town, famed for the Cardinals. While I was teaching there, at Washington University, St. Louis sported a second team, the Blue Jays. However, they were having a hard time making a go of it. To try to boost attendance, complimentary passes were sent to the clergy in town, in the hopes that they would spread the good word.

Now, I have only minimum clerical credentials, and though I had never attended a professional sporting event, who could tell? I slipped the pass into my wallet and forgot all about it. Miraculously, you might say, it was the prefix *Rev.* on my stadium pass that caught the tailor's eye.

"*¿Usted es reverendo?*"

Excitedly, I affirmed, "*Sí, sí, sí.*"

"*¿Qué iglesia?*"

Methodist.

"*¿Metodisto?*" he shouted.

"*Sí, sí, sí,*" we said, echoing his exalted exuberance.

Improbably, or as luck would have it, the tailor was one of twelve Methodists in all of Mexico City. From that point on, things could not have gone more smoothly. The twelve gathered in his home for Sunday-morning worship, and since that was the following day he urged us to join him. Unfortunately, we told him, we had to move on that night to San Miguel. So, smilingly, we shook hands and walked out of the tailor's shop with my boxed-up suit as he happily slipped my personal check into his breast pocket.

MISSING

The next episode in my retelling of the improbables in my life has come to be known in our family as "the Case of the Missing Harp."

A family in Oakland had a daughter who quite out of the blue began to ask for a harp. Her parents bought her an inexpensive one and told her that if she practiced conscientiously they would buy her a better one. Her diligence exceeded their expectations, so they bought a harp from the world's premier harp maker, in Boulder, Colorado. At the age of fourteen their daughter became a harpist in the Oakland Symphony Orchestra.

The orchestra had a custom that whenever a concert was repeated on the following evening, large instruments were left in a padlocked storage room. On one such occasion, on the second evening the harp could not be found. The concert had to proceed without her.

The girl's family was at an impasse. Then, when the young harpist's grandmother got wind of the loss she began networking with her dowser acquaintances. Together, they came up with the phone number of a psychic in Kansas, to whom the harpist's mother appealed for help. The psychic agreed to pursue the matter but said he had never been to California, never even traveled west of Kansas. He asked to be sent a map of the vicinity in question, and the family did manage to mail him a street map of Oakland, on which they circled the pertinent area.

Several days after receiving the map, the psychic phoned and said that if one traveled west on Highway 580 and turned right onto MacArthur Boulevard, the harp was on the second block, in the last house on the right-hand side of the street.

So once again, the family wondered what to do.

They contacted the police, who informed them that they could not enter the house without a search warrant. A psychic's hunch was not sufficient cause.

In time, friends helped the family devise a plan. They created a flyer and nailed it to telephone poles in a two-block radius around the targeted house. It read: "$300 reward for information leading to the recovery of a lost harp."

Two days later, the mother of the harpist received an anonymous message on her answering machine. The voice said that he did not have the harp but he knew where it was and might be able to get it back into the hands of its rightful owner. Apparently, the caller realized that he had a hot item on his hands and the problem of disposing of a bulky treasure without leaving a traceable clue.

Several more anonymous calls led to this solution.

The caller told the parents of the harpist to stand at the top of the exterior fire escape behind a nearby Safeway store at 9:00 p.m. the following evening. If they did so, they would find the harp intact, safely covered with a black plastic bag, at the front of the fire escape. In the bag was a note saying that the deliverer was not interested in the reward.

Everything proceeded according to plan, and so it transpired that the missing harp was recovered and returned to the young prodigy.

Chapter Thirteen

Primal Religions, Primal Passions

J ohn Collier, one-time United States commissioner of Indian Affairs, said about Native Americans, the indigenous people of North America, "They had what the world has lost, the reverence and passion for human personality, and for the earth and its web of life."

To that double loss, I believe we can add three others. First, we, the nonindigenous peoples of North America, are less clear about our values, what is important in life. Second, we are less able to see the Infinite in the finite, the Transcendent in the immanent. And third, we have lost our way metaphysically, which is to say, we have lost sight of the Great Chain of Being with its multiple levels of reality.

Before proceeding, let me say something about the word

indigenous. Literally, it means only "native," and it is used mainly to refer to fauna and flora in their natural habitats. As the chapter title indicates, however, I am using the word to refer to people — specifically those whose ancestors lived where they themselves are now living. As far as we can trace their lineages, they are not immigrants. On our continent they are the people John Collier was speaking of, the Native Americans. In my experience the principal way in which indigenous people differ from the rest of us is that the lines they draw between the things in this world are not as categorical and sharp as the lines that we draw.

For example, we draw a categorical line between human beings, as the acme of intelligence, and lesser breeds, which is to say, the rest of the animal kingdom. The inference is that animals are markedly less intelligent than we are. Watch that, indigenous peoples have advised me. To the native mind, as is borne out in their myriad myths, the trickster coyote can outsmart human beings.

To illustrate this difference, take the categorical line between animate and inanimate that we draw. My Onondagan friend Oren Lyons told me how his uncle once erased that distinction completely. Oren happened to be the first of his tribe to attend college, and when he returned home during a semester break, he had an encounter with his uncle that changed his life.

"Once, when I went home during a college vacation," he told me, "my uncle took me on a fishing trip. When we were in the middle of the lake he said to me, 'Oren, you've been to college. You must be pretty smart now. Let me ask you a question: Who are you?' "

Oren was stunned. He asked, "What do you mean, Uncle? You know me. I'm your nephew."

His uncle was not satisfied, and simply repeated his question. "Who are you?"

"I'm Oren Lyons."

"No," his uncle responded.

Oren tried again: "I'm a human being."

"No."

Oren tried again and again. When he had exhausted all the answers he could think of, he said, "I guess I don't know who I am. So tell me, Uncle, who am I?"

His uncle said, "Oren, do you see that bluff over there? You *are* that bluff. Do you see that giant pine on the other shore? You *are* that pine tree. Do you see the water that our boat is floating on? You *are* that water. You are not separate. You *are* the water under the canoe. There is *no* sharp division between human and animal — the coyote trickster can outwit humans in our stories."

Oren nodded, finally understanding that he was much more than his own man. I think of that story every time I hear native people discuss how differently they perceive themselves in relation to nature. They don't divide the world categorically into objects that are separate from one another.

Another story I find revealing about Oren's integrity has to do with the time he spent a grueling day negotiating land claims with a congressman. Afterward they went to a bar and were forced to wait several minutes to be served. The congressman kept looking at his watch until the bar finally opened.

"What will you have?" the politician asked.

Oren said, "Oh, orange juice would be just fine."

"Good," the congressman said, "a screwdriver. I'll be right back."

"No!" Oren objected. "Just *plain orange juice!*"

Well, the congressman brought Oren his orange juice and proceeded to have three martinis. Then his speech began to slur and his steps became uncertain.

Seeing the absurdity of the situation, Oren made the uncanny observation that history was repeating itself *in reverse*, since all the treaties between native people and the American government during the nineteenth century had been signed while kegs of gin and rum and other alcoholic beverages — firewater — were opened and passed around. This time, Oren smiled to himself because the shoe was on the other foot.

SWEAT LODGE

I would like to share a story that combines a rendezvous with one of my students and a Native American ritual.

A graduate student of mine, James Botsford, earned a law degree, thinking it would give him some leverage to change the world for the better. Degree in hand, James sent his résumé to many of the world's most prestigious human rights and environmental organizations. As an afterthought, responding to a job posting in the basement of the law school, he also sent his résumé to a legal aid office in Nebraska that was looking for someone willing to live and work on an Indian reservation as the only Indian legal aid lawyer in the state.

Most of the preeminent international organizations didn't respond at all. Those that did only asked for financial contributions. The tone of the response from the reservation was "How soon can you get here?" In addition to the posted salary of $15,000 a year, they offered $600 for "remote-duty bonus" and the use of a rusty truck. The job was his if he wanted it.

James took the job. He packed up his family's belongings and moved with his wife, Krista, and their infant son, Tenzin, to Indian country.

During the next seven years on the reservation, James had opportunities to cocounsel major Indian rights cases with the Native American Rights Fund (NARF), based in Boulder, Colorado. NARF is the premier Indian rights law firm in the United States, and one of those years James attended a conference as a representative for Indian interests.

Once a year Native American lawyers across the country meet to confer about typical problems they deal with. When they gathered in Berkeley, California, close to where Kendra and I have lived since 1984, we invited James to supper. He was quite eager to share a story about his first traditional sweat, and he didn't seem able to turn his mind to anything else.

"Don't think of it as a sauna, Huston," James corrected me. "It's not like a sauna at all! *It's a true and intense spiritual practice.*"

His enthusiasm whetted my curiosity, and by networking with my Native American contacts I found a trail that led to an upcoming sweat near Palm Springs. I followed the trail and was advised that it was going to be a "ten-bucket sweat," which I learned was as high (or hot) as they come.

The day I arrived I discovered that the participants had been busy all day constructing the lodge, which was about the size and shape of an igloo. The "fireman," as he is known in those circles, tended the fire by heating large rocks so hot that they glowed. It was the first time I had ever seen glowing rocks. When darkness descended, the fireman used reindeer antlers to maneuver the stones into a pit in the center of the lodge. According to custom, we all stripped to our shorts. Then with towels wrapped around ourselves, we entered the low door of the lodge.

Since it was a cool evening, the steam billowing from the glowing rocks as the first three or four buckets of water were thrown onto them felt good. However, things changed dramatically. Every subsequent bucket of water tossed onto the hot stones sent the temperature up ten degrees. The seventh bucket of water made it hard for me to breathe, and I became apprehensive. With the eighth bucket it was so difficult to breathe that I became alarmed; with the ninth I was saying to myself that when the tenth bucket of water hit the rocks I didn't know what I'd do — scream? Plunge for the door flap of the lodge? Who knows?

I looked around the tepee and noticed that the other participants, mostly Native Americans, were calm and collected, despite the suffocating heat and the steam that made it increasingly difficult to breathe. Some of the men began to chant, which I found remarkable, considering the lack of oxygen. My lungs were stinging with the heat, and yet these men could breathe well enough to actually sing. Later, I learned they were offering up their pain and suffering to Wakan-Tanka, to God.

I took the cue from them and sat stock-still, focused on my breath. Slowly, and improbably, I was able to calm down and not make a spectacle of myself.

I learned from the encounter that sweats clear not only the outsides of bodies by opening the pores of the skin but also the insides of bodies as well.

Around 2:00 a.m. I awoke from an unusually deep sleep and stumbled to the toilet (which was simply the great outdoors), where it felt as if I were emptying out in the way rescuers empty the water out of the lungs of someone who has almost drowned. Or to change the metaphor, I felt as if a plumber's friend was being plunged through the entire length of my alimentary canal, cleaning it out in the way a sausage is pushed from its coating.

When I related this in a talk I once gave, a woman in the audience remarked that it was worth her effort to attend the lecture just to hear that comparison.

Still, I have one regret, and it is a serious one.

I was so consumed by the physical severity of the ordeal that I completely forgot that James had insisted that a sweat was intended to be a true and intense *spiritual* experience. That was why my native friends didn't complain and instead offered their pain and suffering up to Wakan-Tanka, as a true and living sacrifice.

In retrospect, I feel sure that it was this, and not the physical severity of the ordeal, that James had in mind when he said that a native sweat should not be reduced or diminished by calling it a mere sauna. First and foremost, James had reminded me, an Indian sweat is a purification ceremony for both the body and the spirit, which is perhaps why the traditional tepee is sometimes called a medicine lodge — "medicine" in the native sense of being a therapeutic approach to curing the whole person that involves religious practice, herbalism, ritual purging, and ceremony.

THE ONONDAGA SEMINAR

In the late 1970s Kendra was asked to lead a youth seminar for two months, during which time a hundred students of various nationalities would travel around the world together, the object being to promote international understanding.

I proposed that the seminar open with a program conducted by the Native Americans who lived nearby, who otherwise would not be encountered during the students' travels. The idea was accepted, so I rounded up two carloads of Onondagans and led them in my own car to the designated spot, a beautiful and spacious sanctuary that was an easy drive north of New York City.

When we arrived I welcomed the members of the seminar, who were seated on the grass. I explained that our opening session would be conducted by the Native Americans I had brought with me. With great respect, the Native Americans all stood up and acknowledged the applause. Then one of them stepped forward while the others sat back down.

This man, around thirty, was unusually tall and an altogether impressive young man. He said that he would like to launch the seminar with a prayer in his native Onondagan tongue.

I was moved by his offer and agreed, then dutifully sat down to listen, bowing my head and closing my eyes, prepared to enter the attitude of prayer that I am accustomed to. But as the prayer stretched on and on, I opened my eyes to see what was going on. The young native was offering up his prayer with his eyes open, which I had never seen before. As he prayed, he kept turning his head side to side and up and down. He continued this unusual behavior for about forty minutes, and I was absolutely mystified.

Finally, he announced — in English — that the seminar was now officially launched, whereupon he walked forward into the crowd to mingle with everyone.

Eventually, the crowd began to disperse and I sought out the young speaker.

"What were you doing during the forty minutes that you were speaking?" I asked.

"I was looking around at this beautiful place, this sanctuary," he said easily, "and named everything in my prayer that I could see — the faces in the audience, the grass they were sitting on, the trees, the water in the nearby pond, the ducks that were swimming on it, the clouds in the sky. I pronounced the names of everything that I could see. I asked the Creator to bless this venture He helped get under way."

Then he added, a beautiful touch, that the indigenous world includes all of creation. There is no such thing as dead matter.

"Stones can bless you as you walk on them," he said, "so you should ask them to bless you."

This Greeting of Thanks to the Natural World attests to this deep attitude of gratitude that many indigenous people maintain:

Greeting and thanks to each other as people.
To the earth, mother of all, greetings and thanks.
To all the water, waterfalls and rains, rivers and
     oceans, greetings and thanks.

To all the fish life, greetings and thanks.
To the grass and greens, beans and berries, as we send
  thanks to the food plants.
Medicine herbs of the world, and their keepers,
greetings and thanks.
To the trees for shelter and shade, fruit and beauty,
  greetings and thanks.
To all birds, large and small, joyful greetings and
  thanks.
And for the four directions, the four winds, thank you
  for purifying the air we breathe and giving us
  strength, greetings.
To thunderers, our grandfathers in the sky,
  we hear your voices — greetings and thanks.
And now the sun for the light of a new day and all
  the fires of life, greetings and thanks.
To our oldest grandmother, the moon, leader of
  women all over the world.
And the stars for their mystery, beauty, and
  guidance, greetings and thanks.
To our teachers from all times, reminding us how
  to live in harmony, greetings and thanks.
And for all the gifts of creation, for all the love
  around us, greeting and thanks.
And for all that is forgotten, we remember with
  our words.
Now our minds are one.

THE MEDICINE

When, in 1990, the Supreme Court outlawed the Native American Church because its sacrament was nonaddictive peyote, a Caucasian with deep pockets financed a journey to Mazatlán, Mexico, flying leaders from more than a dozen tribes, along with a film crew headed by Gary Rhine, of Kifaru Productions. Upon arrival, they were all met by vans that transported them forty miles east to the village of Trebol, and then beyond to a makeshift meeting place in Tarahumara territory that adjoins the land of the Huichol.

I accompanied the group because I was working with them toward the restoration of the church's constitutional religious rights in the United States and because of my respect for one of the oldest religions in the world.

The plan was for the leaders of the Native American Church to conduct four all-night vigils, guided by peyote, the "medicine," the respectful phrase they use to describe the sacred peyote plant. During the day each group planned their strategy for regaining their religious rights to practice their ancient religion when they returned home.

We were joined in our vigils by a small group of Tarahumara Indians, who, I was surprised to learn, had run two hundred miles on sandals made from old car tire treads to participate in the meeting, subsisting only on handfuls of salt. The Tarahumara slept on the ground, out in the open, while we slept in traditional tepees for two nights and then outdoors, in our sleeping bags, for the other two. The Tarahumara had the honor of carrying the sacred peyote medicine for the event, arriving in a state of bliss. Their presence was a source of strength and inspiration for the dozens of other native people who had sacrificed so much to come to the gathering.

The climax of our four-day-long meeting came around four in the morning on the last night. The drums beat loudly but rhythmically, in perfect unison. The Tarahumara men, arm in arm, performed a dance that moved counterclockwise around the bonfire in the center, in a formation that reminded me of the spokes of a wheel. Periodically, the drumming would stop and the men would break ranks and leap wildly into the air like the spirits of deer, the animal incarnation of the peyote medicine. Slowly, the drumming would resume and the men would re-form into the spokes of a rotating cartwheel and begin to dance again.

During my stay in Mazatlán, I learned that one of the favorite Tarahumara sports was a hundred-mile-long race, which lasts more than two days, in which each side kicks a small stone at a grueling pace.

In 1928 the Mexico Olympic Committee sent two Tarahumara runners to Amsterdam to compete in the games. But when the runners discovered that the closing marathon race was "only" 26.2 miles, they concluded that the races were far too short and must have been for women, and they returned home.

When the 1990 contingent returned to the United States, a great Native American leader took over. When I was introduced to him, he held out his hand and quipped, "I'm Reuben Snake, your humble serpent." He succeeded in putting together a coalition that included all of the more than three hundred tribes in the United States — the first time that had ever been done. The judiciary having deserted the Native American Church, the Indians decided to end-run it and take their case to the legislature.

But this meant that the congressmen had to be educated on the issues. Under Reuben's tutelage, a documentary film was produced by Gary Rhine, Phil Cousineau, and James Botsford and was titled *The Peyote Road*. The film was shown on public television and in markets all over the world, plus a short, six-minute version was shown in the halls of Congress. Additionally, a book was created to supplement the film, and Reuben asked me to write it. While the book was still in press, Congress passed the Native American Freedom Restoration Act, which was signed by President Clinton into law in the garden behind the White House.

Thus began a friendship that ended only with Reuben's death

a few years ago, which occurred at the height of an out-of-season thunderstorm that stopped abruptly with Reuben's last breath.

A final note on Reuben, who was my preeminent Native American teacher. One evening, in Santa Fe, New Mexico, Reuben told me, "Huston, our tepees pointed east, and when we stepped out of them in the morning we would throw our arms up in the air and shout *Aho!* when we saw the sun rising on the horizon. Huston, you should do that, too!" And I have done so ever since. To this day, whenever I glimpse the sun in the morning I raise my arms and shout, *Aho!* The first time I see the sun every day infuses me with a sense of rejoicing, as I imagine the sunlight bringing life and joy and beauty.

In 1996 our book appeared under the title *One Nation under God: The Triumph of the Native American Church*, edited by Reuben Snake and Huston Smith.

Chapter Fourteen

Surprised by Existence

When I reached middle age, I still had all my wisdom teeth. However, once when I visited my dentist, he concluded that they were likely to give him more trouble than they would give me pleasure, so he said, "Out with them!"

"We put you under for this," he continued, trying to relax me. Then he held a syringe to my upper arm and told me to count to ten. I remember getting to three.

When I woke up I was in a cramped recovery room and the prototype of the Big Nurse was hovering over me and — I kid you not — she was beating me: *Slap, slap, slap.*

"Come on," I thought. "Life is real, life is earnest, so get on with it and stop this dreaming!"

When I opened my eyes — though she was still beating me, *slap, slap, slap* — my first words were, "It's so beautiful!"

The vision vanished so quickly that even as I said those words I couldn't remember *what* was so beautiful, but the memory of *how* beautiful it was remains with me to this very day.

Later, I told the story to Kimberly, one of our daughters, and she said that the same thing had happened to her. When she awoke from some anesthesia that had been administered to her for another kind of operation, she heard herself blurting to one of the nurses, "I love you."

Later, during one of my lectures, I mentioned these two episodes, and a woman in the audience raised her hand and said that the same thing had happened to her. She had been thrown from a horse and landed on her head, a fall that resulted in a slight concussion. Upon regaining consciousness, she found herself exclaiming, "I'm so happy!"

What are we to make of all this? What were the referents of those three exclamations — beauty, love, and joy?

Obviously these exclamations referred to nothing in the contextual world, so my first theory was that the medication we received bypassed the ostensible referents and plunged straight for the souls of the subjects. Those "fountains are ever on," the first-century philosopher Plotinus wrote, from which everything in the subjects' lives issue forth.

However, a little pondering prompted a different hypothesis. Perhaps the medication had somehow peeled off the subjects' lifetimes of habituation, and we were experiencing what infants see when they first open their eyes, namely *existence, the world, what's out there*, but with an adult understanding. Would it not appear incredibly beautiful and elicit feelings of love and joy?

To help emphasize the point and back myself up on this interpretation, I will call on William Wordsworth and his poem

"Ode on Intimations of Immortality from Recollections of Early Childhood":

> There was a time when meadow, grove, and stream,
> The earth, and every common sight,
>> To me did seem
>> apparell'd in celestial light,
> The glory and the freshness of a dream.
> It is not now as it hath been of yore; —
>> Turn whereso'er I may,
>> By night or day.
> The things which I have seen I now can see no more.

A friend of mine once told me that as an adolescent, he found that he could regain a dream if he bent over and observed the world upside down through his spread legs. But the trick only worked for a day or two before his mind caught on to it.

Thus to my satisfaction, at least, I have identified the referent of the three honorific encomiums that I cited: *beauty*, *love*, and *joy*. They describe Existence in primal pristine glory, which habituation has not blurred.

THE I CHING

The *I Ching*, or *Book of Changes*, was not in evidence during my childhood in China. But when I began to teach comparative philosophy and religion, the translation by Richard Wilhelm had recently been published and the classic work suddenly jumped to prominence in my life.

The *I Ching* rings the changes of life on hexagrams, six horizontal lines, half of them divined, the other half not, for a total of sixty-four possible combinations. There are two ways to obtain the reading for a particular consultation. The time-saving way is to use three coins of the lowest combination, which in the West would be pennies, for the oracle hugs the earth and shuns aristocracy. If, let's say, all three coins turn up as heads, the first and lowest line is unbroken. But if the faces of the coins are not identical, the line is broken. One repeats the procedure until all six lines are in place.

The *I Ching* is the world's most democratic oracle. Its messages do not come from on high or from outside, as they did with the Delphic Sibyls. Rather, they emerge from oneself and the circumstances that one happens to be in. Having described the time-saving way to consult the oracle, I will turn now to the formal way. I will not describe this way in detail, except to say that it is reverential.

This way consists of using yarrow stalks, the commonest weed in the world, which again signifies earthiness and democracy. Wash or, more ideally, bathe, and dress as if you were welcoming a guest. Light a candle. Formulate a question, or rather an issue. The oracle does not give yes-or-no answers. Ponder the issue for a few minutes.

Then, seated on a pad on the floor, pick up the fifty yarrow stalks that you have gathered. Place one stalk at the head of your pad. From that place of honor it will preside over what is going to happen. Divide the remaining stalks into two piles, and place one stalk between the fourth and little fingers of each hand. Keeping them there, pick up half of the remaining stalks and remove them, two at a time. If one remains, the bottom line is unbroken. Repeat the process until all six lines are in place. Then consult the *I Ching* manual for the reading or interpretation.

When a sinologist was explaining the *I Ching* (customarily contracted to merely "I," pronounced like "ee") to one of my classes, the one-hour time limit forced him to use the abbreviated method that employs coins. They came up with the first hexagram

— all six lines unbroken. That is the best hexagram of all: "Creative Power. The time is exceptional in inspiration, energy, and will."

Of course, my students were intrigued. A handful of them asked if they could have an evening session in one of their apartments and be introduced to the formal way of consulting the *I*. The sinologist agreed, and when we were ready to begin he explained the formal procedure and had six of the twelve students throw the yarrow stalks and build the hexagram. It turned out to be the same one the coins had come up with during our morning class. The odds against this are very high. But wait, there's more.

My wife, Kendra, is a therapist. The counseling center she once worked at assigned her to work with a very disturbed young woman. The woman arrived in a sari and sat on the floor with a copy of the *I Ching* manual. The hexagram it had come up with did not please her, and she wanted Kendra to throw the coins. Kendra did, and they came up with the same hexagram the woman had drawn: "Hexagram 18. REPAIR: The object of your inquiry is in a state of disrepair. This may be an inherited difficulty, or it may have come about because you are unaware of the need to monitor and analyze the details of the situation. Too many elements in your life have reached a state of neglect and disrepair."

Continuing to be displeased, the client demanded another throw. Kendra obliged, and uncannily enough, the same hexagram surfaced.

Later, we asked a friend of ours who is a mathematician about this, and she said that the chances of this sequence occurring were infinitesimal.

WHAT WE EXPERIENCE WHEN WE DIE

Surprisingly, we know what we experience when we die. The answer appears in a Tibetan book titled *Bardothodal*. *Bardo* is literally "place," but it refers not to a geographical place. More accurately, it translates as "experience." *Thodol* means unequivocally "dead." For these reasons, the book title that has come down to us is *The Tibetan Book of the Dead*.

What the book tells us is that after a human body dies, its final destination is a place or dimension called "the Pure Light of the Void," which is eternal and far above any happiness we can experience on earth. However, depending on the individual's karma, intermediate states must be traversed. These resemble what we experience in this world, and being familiar, the subject is tempted to slide off into them. The *Bardothodol* sternly warns against doing that, however, for it would derail the soul and prolong its journey to the Clear Light. Like a coach, the book rallies the subject to continue on its journey: "Oh nobly born, press on. Do not be afraid. Be strong. Keep going." When fearful, daunting visions appear, the *bardo* tells the subject do not be afraid. They are only projections of the subject's own mind and should be disregarded. The bulk of the book consists of descriptions of what those with residues of karma that must be worked off must experience as they make their way to the eternal, unimaginably blissful beatitude that will in due course be everybody's home.

The *Bardothodal* is an exciting, bracing, exhilarating, and reassuring book. It not only enlightens us but reassures us as it indicates what lies ahead for us all.

Chapter Fifteen

What's It All About?

The poet T. S. Eliot loved to tell a story about his lifelong sparring partner, Bertrand Russell, an outspoken atheist.

One day in London, Eliot flagged down a cab, and driving off the cabbie glanced back at him and said, "You're T. S. Eliot, ain't you?"

Eliot acknowledged that he was and asked the cabbie how he knew.

"Aye, but I have an eye for celebrity," the cabbie replied in a distinctive cockney accent. "Why, just last week Lord Russell was sitting where you are, and I said to him, "Well, Bertie, what's it all about? And you know what? He couldn't tell me."

Actually, it's quite easy to say what it's all about.

Two things. First, it's about trying to discern and understand reality — as much of existence as our human faculties are capable of comprehending. The everyday view is limited to what we perceive, plus what empirical science adds to this.

However, this overlooks metaphysics, the science of the multiple levels of reality that Arthur Lovejoy catalogued in his classic study, *The Great Chain of Being*. In that chain, the links descend from the Infinite, down through successively smaller links to the final one, which barely escapes being nothing at all.

The second thing that "it's all about" is trying to figure out how, with the help of insights from our philosophical and religious traditions, we can best live our lives within the inclusive context just referred to.

There's another way of saying what it's all about, and having mentioned Eliot and Russell, I will now invoke Robert Oppenheimer. He tells of coming upon a clutch of teenagers who were working their way through the Bible and had come to Ecclesiastes.

"Don't you find Ecclesiastes difficult?" Oppenheimer asked.

"Oh, it's very difficult. But what we don't understand we explain to each other."

Oppenheimer cited that as a quip, but actually it is simply a straightforward description of human life. Each of us knows very little of what we need to know, so we ask our companions. And thus begins the process by which we proceed to understand as much as we can of what it's all about.

I'm reminded here of my great friend the Winnebago-Hunkpapa Road Man, Reuben Snake, who said, "We are all brothers walking arm in arm down the road of life together, so we should help each other along that road."

OF PRIMARY IMPORTANCE

My mind often goes back to an interview that was conducted with Peter Drucker, dean of management consultants, when he retired.

Toward the close of the interview the interlocutor said, "Peter, it's not too much to cite you as the founder of the now flourishing management consulting industry. The coverage of your retirement has been saturating the airwaves and the press. However, there's one question I haven't heard anyone ask you, and I will put it to you now. Is there anything in your career that you wish had happened that didn't happen?"

Drucker thought for a moment and then said, "Actually, there *is* something that I wish had happened but never did."

"I am sitting in the office of the company's CEO, for the wrap-up session. We have spent two weeks together examining every aspect of the company's operations that we could think of and are reviewing what we have accomplished. What I wish had happened but never did is that the CEO, now my friend, would have leaned back in his chair and said, 'Peter, you haven't told me a thing I didn't know.'"

Drucker added, "That's invariably the case. I never tell my clients anything they didn't already know. I take it to be my job to point out that what they have been dismissing as of secondary importance is actually of primary importance."

The reason this scene keeps coming back to me is the way it applies to my own life. How often do I stop to ask myself if what I am doing is really what I ought to be doing at that moment?

ONLY CONNECT

It could be argued that since the Middle Ages no ideology — not even Marxism — has been as influential in the interpretation of literature, art, sports, and above all biography as the psychological theory of Sigmund Freud. This theory posits that infant sexuality is the motor of child development, and that fear of castration, or for women the fear of having been castrated, fuels that theory.

What trickled into popular thinking is that sexual and aggressive impulses, like the engine in a steam engine, must not be dammed up but have an outlet. Antagonism toward parents of the same sex is only natural. So what we got is *Playboy* magazine, and in California a commune where members were dedicated to racking up as many orgasms as possible, all in the name of mental health.

In the 1970s, it was considered therapeutic to "let it all hang out," in the name of authenticity, without regard for the wounded self-esteem of others. A minority of parents tried ultrapermissiveness in the belief that restraining sexual and aggressive impulses would cause neuroses, but the experiment proved unsuccessful, and the pendulum swung back toward a centrist position.

One afternoon, in the early 1950s, Aldous and Laura Huxley invited Kendra and me to tea, allowing me to ask Aldous a question I had always wanted to ask him: "Are there any books that you have gone back to read again?"

"There were two," he said. "Herbert Read's *Art and Education*, and *The Origins of Love and Hate*, by Ian Suttie." The second of these two books is the one that concerns me here.

Ian Suttie was a research scientist and psychoanalyst who focused on infants' earliest responses to life, and to this end he shot innumerable reels of films documenting the earliest activities of infants. Running, rerunning, and analyzing those films he reached the conclusion that when infants become aware, their first act is to reach out for something to hold on to and bond or connect with. They will gaze endlessly at their mothers' faces bent adoringly over them. In a day or two they will respond. Faint traces of smiles will appear on their lips, and soon these will blossom into full-fledged smiles. And the process continues. After a day or two infants will drop the nipple and break out into gurgles and chortles.

Suttie concluded from all this that Freud was right in recognizing (it might not be too much to say discovering) that our minds have what he called a "keystone," regions that we are not consciously aware of. But he was wrong in positing sex and aggression as life's engines.

Toward the end of his life, the novelist E. M. Forster drew on this for his parting advice to humanity: "Only connect."

For it is true that we are like theater tickets that read: *"Not good if detached."*

THE GOOD NEWS

As of this writing, in the fall of 2011, the world is suffering a deep financial recession. The news of it is on everyone's mind. There is some good news, however, no matter how seldom it is heard, and here is some of it:

Never in recorded history has there been less starvation.

Never in recorded history has there been less slavery.

Never in recorded history have so many human beings lived under rulers that they themselves elected.

Never in recorded history has the position of women been as good as it is today.

Slowly, but surely, it is coming to be recognized that torture is never in order and should never be countenanced.

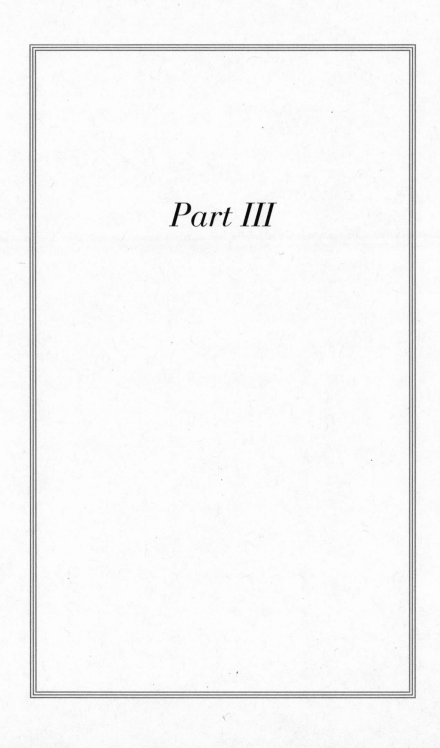

Part III

Chapter Sixteen

Fame at My Elbow

I n this last part of the book I would like to offer a gallery of brief portraits of notable people I have encountered in my life. I begin with Gerald Heard, historian and philosopher, said by many to be the best-kept secret of the twentieth century. Heard occasioned one of the two conversions I have undergone in my life. The first of these was my conversion from the world of practical affairs to the life of the mind, when I was a graduate student. The second was an overnight experience when I read his masterpiece, *Pain, Sex, and Time: A New Outlook on Evolution and the Future of Man*. The book converted me from the scientific worldview, which takes the visible world to be the only world there is, to the vaster world of the mystics.

I am in good company in owing that conversion to Gerald

Heard. Aldous Huxley credited Heard with converting him from the cynical nihilism of his *Brave New World* to the mysticism of *The Perennial Philosophy*.

My peripeteia, as the ancient Greeks called such a sudden and dramatic change of heart or circumstances, occurred when I was a graduate student and was struggling with the problem of pain in the dissertation I was writing. I hadn't given the subject much thought, so I went to the university library and checked out three books on the subject. Back in my room after supper I found my hand gravitating to the one with the most interesting title, *Pain, Sex, and Time*. It took only a few pages to realize that it had nothing to do with my dissertation, but I kept reading. And reading. When dawn broke I was living in the new world that has housed me ever since.

Still, I determined that the book had so radically changed my point of view that I wouldn't read anything else written by Heard until after I received my degree. Once I had my PhD in hand, I vowed, I would read everything he had ever written.

REREADING HEARD

Until very recently, nearly sixty years later, I had not returned to Heard's book for fear that I would find it disappointing. We all know that what affects us at one time may not do so later, for one can't step into the same river twice. I suspect that I might never have reread it, had the invitation to write a foreword not provided the needed excuse for interrupting other duties. I am glad it did, for the rereading has not disappointed me. It is a very good book that withstands the passage of time admirably. But before I say more about the book I should say something more about its author.

Today almost no one has heard of Gerald Heard, but in the second quarter of the twentieth century the situation was otherwise; he was a well-known British polymath. He began his career as a science commentator for the BBC, and H. G. Wells was widely quoted as saying that he was the only one he bothered to listen to on the "wireless." Heard's remarkable early trilogy of academic books included *The Ascent of Humanity* (1929), *The Social Substance of Religion* (1931), and *The Source of Civilization* (1935). *Pain, Sex, and Time* came out in 1939, and in 1941 he wrote the most successful detective story of the day, *A Taste for Honey*, which sold more than half a million copies, an astronomical number in those days. Thirty more books poured forth after that.

In *Pain, Sex, and Time* Heard describes how science deals with *what* happens and sidesteps any *why* questions, and he maintains that a complete account must include them. So with the wisdom of hindsight we can say that the object of the evolutionary process seems to have been to produce bodies with minds. When these advance to self-consciousness the mind becomes free. No longer defined by antecedent causes, it can take charge of its future.

The evolution of the human body has been completed, but it possesses two properties that suggest that its mind can continue to evolve. One of these is its inordinate sensitivity to pain, and the other is human sexuality, which is not contained by periodicity and is permanently available. The surplus vitality that these properties token suggests that in humanity the life force is pressing like a jack-in-the-box for the release that mental evolution could afford. Rudiments of such evolution can be spotted in historical times in the increasing acuity of human vision and our ability to distinguish more bands in the color spectrum, but real evolution will be in the ability of consciousness to break out of individual pockets — packets, I almost wrote — and phase into God's infinite consciousness. This is more than a theoretical possibility. Mystics are the advance scouts of humankind who have transcended their egos and in exceptional cases merged with God completely. One more point. Methods for effecting this breakout are solidly in place. They are the spiritual techniques of yoga, meditation, and prayer.

This is the vision that took me over on that fate-filled night when I first read this book, and my pulse still quickens as I bring it to mind. But the brief account of it that I have given here doesn't come close to indicating what an interesting book it is. Heard constructs his thesis from an awesome data bank, and even those who do not find the thesis convincing will find the book bristling with obscure scientific and historical facts that keep the pages turning. Some of the facts have been disproved, but enough of them remain to make the thesis still credible. If it was strong enough to persuade Huxley, I for one am still not going to dismiss it out of hand.

In 1949, while living in Denver and about to move to St. Louis, I decided to try to meet Gerald before moving farther east. I got the address of his monastery in Trabuco Canyon from his publisher and set out hitchhiking to Southern California.

As I was saying good-bye to him at his monastery, he said, "Have you met Aldous Huxley? He likes to meet people who share our interests." With that, he scribbled Huxley's phone number on a scrap of paper and handed it to me.

When I reached Los Angeles I called the number. A house sitter answered and told me that Huxley and his wife, Maria, were at their cabin hideaway in the Mojave Desert. I was given their phone number there, and when I called it, Aldous answered. He said he would be happy to receive me and told me to take the next bus to Barstow. He said that after about twenty minutes I would see their cabin on my left, the only one in sight. He would be seated on the porch.

All this happened according to plan, and after I helped Maria sweep the sand out of their cabin, Aldous took me for a long walk through the barren stretches of the Mojave. He said he loved the desert because of its symbolic power — the emptiness emptied his mind.

On the twenty-fifth anniversary of Huxley's death, the *Los Angeles Times* asked me to write a commemorative essay, and this is what I wrote.

REMEMBERING ALDOUS HUXLEY

There was a moment in the 1950s when there was talk of pooling the talents of Aldous Huxley, Igor Stravinsky, and Martha Graham to turn *The Tibetan Book of the Dead* into a ballet with Greek chorus.

That moment passed, but when Aldous Huxley died a quarter-century ago this week [on November 22, 1963], it was the words of that Tibetan manual that were read into his ear by his prior request: "Now there is approaching that clear white light of the Void. Do not be afraid. *Do not be afraid.* It is your friend. Go fearlessly into that Light of the Void" (abridged).

It was likewise of the Void that Huxley spoke most during my first meeting with him in 1947. He and his wife, Maria, were at their cabin hide-away in the Mojave Desert, and Aldous took me for a long walk through its barren stretches.

He loved the desert, he told me, for its symbolic power. Its emptiness emptied his mind. "The boundlessness of its sands [I paraphrase] spreads a mantle of sameness — hence unity — over the world's multiplicity in something of the way snow does. The Nothingness to which the Desert Fathers were drawn is not a blank negation. It is a no-thing-ness in which everything is so interfused that divisions are transcended. Pure light contains all the frequencies of the rainbow, but undemarcated. The Void is the vacuum-plenum complex, grasped by its vacuum pole."

Years later, when I helped to bring Huxley to Massachusetts Institute of Technology for the 1960 fall semester, the audience for his public lectures grew until by mid-point in the series, the Boston Police Department had to augment its staff on Wednesday evenings to handle the traffic jams that stretched from Cambridge all the way across the Charles River. When I alluded to this as a tribute, Huxley disclaimed it characteristically. "It's because I've been around so long," he said. "I've become like Queen Anne's Cottage. If I live to be a hundred, I shall be like Stonehenge."

He didn't live to be a hundred, and the world was poorer for his (by current reckoning) relatively early death at age 69. Most obviously, it lost an encyclopedic intelligence. That adjective is overworked these days, but in his case, it comes close to being accurate. When a leading newspaper felt that the *Encyclopedia Britannica* should itself be brought under review in its 14th Edition, no one was surprised when Huxley was asked to do the job. (He found it inferior to the 11th Edition.)

More impressive than the range of the man's mind, however, was its sympathy and interest. Few major intelligences since William James have been as open. Huxley's regard for mysticism was well known by dint of being so nearly notorious. What some overlooked was his equal interest in the workaday world and its exigencies: peace, the population explosion, and conservation of our natural resources. To those who, greedy for transcendence, deprecated the mundane, he advised that we "make the best of both worlds." To their opposites, the positivists, his message was the same, but worded differently: "Fair enough: one world at a time. But not half a world!"

His wit was incisive. Alan Watts happened to pass through Cambridge during Huxley's MIT term, and when I discovered that these two articulate Californians had not met, I arranged a supper to introduce them. Alan had to leave early for a lecture somewhere, and when Huxley and I resumed our seats, there was a pause during which I could almost hear him sorting things out. Then his verdict. "What a curious man. Half monk, and half racetrack operator."

(When I reported this assessment to Alan some months later he loved it, and acknowledged its accuracy.)

It wasn't Huxley's wit alone, of course, that powered his talk — he was a master conversationalist generally. His imposing height, magnificent profile, and sonorous voice all contributed, but it was the way he used words to shape ideas that accounted for the magic. I have been in restaurants where surrounding tables fell silent as their occupants strained to overhear Huxley's words. I seldom left his presence without feeling recharged, as if some new corner of the world — if not new vistas of being — had opened before me.

Accepting the fact that "truth lies at the bottom of a very muddy well," he descended: to ESP and LSD, to "sight without glasses" and Vedanta. But never as embattled renegade — there wasn't a grain of *Invictus* in him. If toward the end he lost his reputation among highbrows, it was not for his omnivorous interests, but because he wasn't content simply to do what he could do well. His competence bored him. So the master of words moved on to what eludes words, remarking over his shoulder that "language is a device for taking the mystery out of reality." Not needing triumph, adulation, or disciples, he could bypass them for truth.

He could bypass them because he had so little egoism. A supreme unpretentiousness characterized him to the end, which came on the same day when John F. Kennedy was assassinated. "It's rather embarrassing," he said, "to have been concerned with the human problem all one's life and find that one has little more to offer by way of advice than, " 'Try to be a little kinder.' " If, as he had earlier observed, the central technique for man to learn is "the art of obtaining freedom from the fundamental human disability of egoism," Huxley achieved that freedom.

But that was not his supreme achievement, for his personal problem was not pride but pessimism. "Did anything more than usually disastrous happen last night," he asked one morning as he approached the breakfast table where I was glancing at the paper. And underlying the world's disasters was its vanity, the seeming meaninglessness of it all — "tomorrow, and tomorrow, and tomorrow, creeps in this petty pace from day to day." His final victory, therefore, lay not in emerging selfless but in winning through to equanimity — an evenness of spirit and generalized good cheer. Thereby the line he used to close his best novel *Brave New World* became the appropriate epitaph for his own life's journey: "Of such is the Kingdom of Heaven."

Said this time without sarcasm.

MORE MEMORIES OF HUXLEY

The Times restricted the space I was allowed, but because of his importance in my life, I want to add several memories of Huxley that crowd my mind. Huxley's wit was incisive and appeared to be almost instinctive. On the first occasion that he and his wife invited us to tea, knowing of my China background, Aldous asked me if the Chinese tea lapsang oolong was just a brand name or had a meaning that could be translated into English. When I said I did not know, he said, "It's probably the Chinese translation of Lipton's."

In my final meetings with Aldous I found all the attributes that I have mentioned were subordinate to the realization of what a good man he was. And since writing that sentence I have come across something that may help to explain why he was as good as he was. While he was conducting a month's retreat at Trabuco College (a kind of improvised monastery) he wrote seven meditations, and I will reproduce the first of them, entitled "Being," here.

God *is*. That is the primordial fact. It is in order that we may discover this fact for ourselves, by direct experience, that we exist. The final end and purpose of every human being is the unitive knowledge of God's being.

What is the nature of God's being? The invocation to the Lord's Prayer gives us the answer. "Our Father which *art* in heaven." God is, and is ours — immanent in each sentient being, the life of all lives, the spirit animating every soul. But this is not all. God is also the transcendent creator and Law-Giver, the Father who loves and, because He loves, also educates His children. And finally, God is "in heaven." That is to say, He possesses a mode of existence which is incommensurable and incompatible with the mode of existence possessed by human beings in their natural, unspiritualized condition. Because He is ours and immanent, God is very close to us. But because He is also in heaven, most of us are very far from God. The saint is one who is as close to God as God is close to him.

It is through prayer that men come to the unitive knowledge of God. But the life of prayer is also a life of mortification, of dying to self. It cannot be otherwise; for the more there is of self, the less there is of God. Our pride, our anxiety, our lusts for power and pleasure are God-eclipsing things. So too is that greedy attachment to certain creatures which passes too often for unselfishness and should be called not altruism but alter-egoism. And hardly less God-eclipsing is the seemingly self-sacrificing service which we give to any cause or ideal that falls short of the divine. Such service is always idolatry, and makes it impossible for us to worship God as we should, much less to know Him. God's kingdom cannot come unless we begin by making our human kingdoms go. Not only the mad and obviously evil kingdoms, but also the respectable ones — the kingdoms of the scribes and pharisees, the good citizens and pillars of society, no less than the kingdoms of the publicans and sinners. God's being cannot be known by us, if we choose to pay our attention and our allegiance to something else, however creditable that something else may seem in the eyes of the world.

As I have said, reading that meditation helps me understand why Huxley was the good man that he was.

VIGNETTES

While I was teaching religion at Washington University in St. Louis, the German painter and sculptor Max Beckman taught at the school of art. He lived for a while in the same building as I did, and I can remember watching him look out the window one dark winter evening standing stock-still, hat jammed down on his head, just looking.

At what? I wondered, then and now.

All I could see were two telephone wires against a background of dark clouds. In his mind's eye he was obviously seeing much more, and how I wished I could see what he did.

Some years later, when I was teaching at Denver University, I was at lunch and sat next to Robert Oppenheimer, the theoretical physicist and to many the "father of the atomic bomb." Concerned about the consequences of the bomb, the production of which he had orchestrated, Oppenheimer had formed, along with Albert Einstein, Enrico Fermi, and others, the Union of Concerned Scientists.

While I was teaching at Denver University I oversaw a small fund to bring stimulating speakers discharged from the army, and a then-unknown songwriter and musician, Pete Seeger, offered to perform for free to help get his act off the ground. He responded quickly to my invitation, and I signed him on.

Listening to him sing before the small last-minute audience, I knew I was in the presence of a winner. I didn't know then what the world was soon to learn, that Pete had a passion for justice, and his songs allowed that passion to surface.

That afternoon turned out to be the start of a friendship, which I have come to learn is the ideal way to befriend a performer destined to become famous. For then they know you are not trafficking on their fame to raise your public image and are a real friend. So Pete became our friend and often stayed with us when he was on the performance circuit, passing through town on a solo tour, or singing with the Weavers. I can still fondly recall him singing "All the Pretty Little Horses," "This Land Is Your Land," "Little Boxes," and other great folk songs to our children at bedtime.

Washington University, in St. Louis, where I taught for many years, was founded by a group of men that included T. S. Eliot's grandfather. On its fiftieth anniversary the grandson and famous poet was invited to give the major address. For him to attend, he had to fly from England, but Eliot consented to do so with one stipulation — that he receive the Eucharist each morning. To help him fulfill this requirement, I chauffeured him to the neighboring Episcopal church, where at 8:00 a.m. he knelt at the railing and received the holy sacraments. Over the course of Eliot's visit I made it a point not to intrude on his privacy.

Martin Luther King Jr. was the leader of the humanitarian surge that led to the passage of the civil rights legislation of the 1960s. CORE (Committee on Racial Equality) was a part of that surge, and Kendra and I were members of its St. Louis chapter. Every Monday evening we met to map out our activities for that week. A white woman would order a meal in a restaurant, and after she had taken a bite or two would wave a black woman to her table as her friend. When the black woman was ordered to leave, the white woman would pay for her uneaten lunch and leave with her.

Sit-ins were staged at lunch counters near the entrances to large stores. Invariably, our interracial group was told to leave, and we would always do so because diplomacy and nonviolence were working principles of CORE. But it was also one of our principles that we would not actually leave until we had forced them to tell us why we must leave; once we heard the reason we would demand to speak to the person who had established the policy. After about two years of sit-ins and negotiations with managers, most of St. Louis's lunch counters were integrated. Then came the time to integrate restaurants and swimming pools, which took longer.

During those years I was the only professor in the St. Louis chapter of CORE, so I was delegated to integrate Washington University. I phoned Dr. King and asked him if he would help us. He agreed to do so but said he did not fly and preferred trains. So he took the train to St. Louis, and I met him at the train station. He was alone with no handlers in those days. I wasn't going to risk the life of the great civil rights leader by driving him myself, so I hailed a taxi. I sat quietly in the backseat of a taxi with him for the forty-minute drive to the university because I had resolved not to intrude on his privacy. When we arrived at the auditorium he gave a stirring address to a turn-away crowd.

After Dr. King's rousing address, we took the same taxi back to the train station. Neither the ride to the university nor the ride back to the station seemed appropriate times to mention to him that I was the son-in-law of Henry Nelson Wieman, the theologian at Boston University whom Dr. King had written his doctoral dissertation on. In that paper he compared the theologies of Wieman and Reinhold Niebuhr and wrote that of the two he found Wieman's ideas more helpful as he pursued his vocation.

The following fall, Washington University opened its doors to African Americans.

AN AFTERNOON WITH BILL WILSON

In 2010 I was asked to write the foreword to a collection of essays and interviews about forgiveness and atonement. Since these two issues are core teachings of Alcoholics Anonymous, I have been prompted to think about Bill Wilson, its founder.

Years ago, I hosted Gerald Heard for a semester at Washington University. One day, he was contacted by his old friend Bill Wilson, who was to deliver an address to a gathering of Alcoholics Anonymous members in Kansas City. Since they wanted to see each other I drove Heard across the state to meet Wilson, and we spent the afternoon with Wilson in his hotel room before he was escorted to dinner and his lecture. One thing remains with me about that afternoon, and it is Wilson's story about a mind-altering mescaline experience he had had. He expressed deep surprise at how closely it resembled the experience — the epiphany — the sudden light that had brought him to his knees and led him to found AA.

WERNER HEISENBERG

As a young professor at Washington University, I was assigned to be the recorder at a conference on science and human responsibility that Chancellor Arthur Compton convened. I relished the idea because I had determined when I was doing my graduate work at the University of Chicago, in the early 1940s, that I would dedicate my life to helping reconcile two of the most potent forces in human history, science and religion.

The idea behind the conference was to gather scientists whose discoveries had created a more dangerous world and ask them to reflect together on what responsibilities their work imposed on them.

One of the scientists we invited was Werner Heisenberg, who had won the 1932 Nobel Prize in Physics but whose work also had led to the atomic bomb.

On the final evening of the conference there was a farewell banquet followed by chamber music. Two violinists and a cellist were imported from the St. Louis Philharmonic Orchestra.

Midway through the concert the great physicist sat down at the piano and played with the string quartet, sight-reading the sheet set before him.

THE ONLY GENIUS I HAVE KNOWN

When MIT decided to add philosophy to its humanities department I was interviewed to chair that department. Noam Chomsky was on the committee that interviewed me. He didn't say a word. In retrospect, I regard him as the only genius I have known.

His seminal discovery was the *universal grammar of language*. To make sense of the world, the human brain is hardwired for sentences with subjects, predicates, tenses, and the like. To cite a single example, when a child begins to talk, he or she says, "I will sing you a song." Never I will *sung* you a song."

To that epochal discovery, I always add Noam's passion for justice. He was a lone voice in denouncing Indonesia's takeover of Timor. He initiated the decision to shift the War Department's contract to manufacture napalm from MIT to the A. D. Little Company. And as of this writing, after the death of the single love of his life, whenever he receives an invitation to speak, at home or abroad, he tells his secretary to tell them to send him his ticket and he will come, for it will give him yet another platform to denounce injustice.

THE POET

When I moved from Washington University to MIT I took on some responsibilities, including the organization of public events. One speaker who stands out in my memory is the English poet and mythographer Robert Graves, who was invited to spend a full month on campus. His public lecture was titled "Forty Hundred Iron Horsemen," that being the number of undergraduates at

MIT. During the question period Graves was asked why he chose to live in Mallorca.

"Because you can get good bread there," he answered.

An invitation went out to the various departments around campus suggesting that they could invite Graves to dinner in the faculty dining room. The philosophy department, where I was ensconced, took the institute up on its offer.

After the meal, Graves pushed his chair back and asked, "What do you gentlemen have against ghosts?"

I thought our chairman, Hillary Putnam, would choke on his brandy. But he recovered himself and changed the subject, saying, "Mr. Graves, I love your love poetry."

The conversation soon switched to Graves's war experience. He recounted being trapped in a burning tank of the fusiliers, in which he served in World War I. When we exclaimed that it must have been terrifying, Graves said, "On the contrary. It was ecstatic."

THE DREAM JOB

In the mid-1950s, the early years of what is now PBS, I was given the dream assignment of mounting a series titled *The Search for America*, in which I conducted one-hour interviews with sixteen people of my choice.

One of my favorite guests on the show was Eleanor Roosevelt. She was quite old then, and when she came down the stairs at NBC and assumed her seat beside me she sat close to me onstage, next to my right elbow. She looked so haggard that I wondered if she could withstand a half hour under the klieg lights, which in those days of television filming were required. I needn't have worried. The moment the cameras started to roll, she leaned forward, and her face became wonderfully animated. She was impressively articulate. I realized as I interviewed her that she had learned how to pace herself, to mete out her limited energy. Since then I have often thought of her unique self-discipline as I have had to learn to pace myself.

Interviewing the theologian Reinhold Niebuhr was like throwing a newspaper into an electric fan. My questions came back to me shredded by nuances and distinctions. The focus of my interview was the idea of historical progress, the myth of the unstoppable power of modernity.

"Is the myth of progress true?" I asked him.

"No," he said, then paused.

"There are *pockets* of progress," he finally said, nuancing his categorical answer.

"Like what?" I had to ask.

"Oh, plumbing and dentistry," he came back. "But net progress, no. Every step forward is followed by sliding backward. We invent DDT and we think we have solved the food shortage. But then thirty years later we are confronted with Rachel Carson's *Silent Spring*. We crack the atom and think that we have solved the energy problem, but then along comes the atomic bomb with its mushroom cloud."

As an illustration of the sweeping influence of Niebuhr's thought, I have heard that there was a moment in the early 1960s when John F. Kennedy, Fidel Castro, and Che Guevara were all reading, at approximately the same time, Niebuhr's *Moral Man and Immoral Society: A Study of Ethics and Politics*, the book that has been deemed the most influential political book of the twentieth century. A tantalizing coincidence, if true, but I have no way to verify that claim.

Another eminent guest on the television show was the economist John Kenneth Galbraith. For that interview I took a film crew to his home. His two young boys met me at the door with their heads covered by paper sacks with holes cut out for them to see through.

"You're here to interview Dad," they said, in unison. "But all you guys do is talk, talk, talk, and that's so boring. So we're here to make it more exciting."

And with that, they adjusted the paper sacks and brandished their toy pistols.

THE POWER OF MYTH

Joseph Campbell was a lifelong friend of mine. His epical achievement was to point out, in *The Power of Myth*, the six-part television series he did with Bill Moyers, that myths have two sides. They can be inspiring and true, but they can also be destructively false. During World War II, Hitler's myth of a super race had all but derailed the word *myth* itself, and Joe's great accomplishment was to get the word back on track and remind us of the psychological truths that myth offers.

One incident centering on Campbell illustrates his contribution.

After Elmer Greene made his reputation on developing biofeedback, he became interested in fringe phenomena. A number of Asian gurus were offering workshops on how their brand of yoga could increase a person's energy. Elmer invited a number of them to the Menninger Clinic in Topeka, Kansas, where he mounted a five-day symposium on the subject of human energy. For reasons that escape me, Joseph Campbell and I were both invited.

During the conference people began to notice that Joe seemed to have more energy than the vaunted yogis. On the evening he spoke, his lecture began at 7:00 p.m., and he didn't let the audience off the hook until 11:00. His parting remark was that he was good for another four hours if anyone in the audience was interested. There were no takers.

The next day someone asked Campbell what *his* yoga was. They wanted to know what gave him so much energy. Joe brushed the question aside, saying that he had no traditional yoga. *His* yoga was reading books. But then he did a double take.

"Come to think of it," he said, "I guess I do have a yoga. It has three parts: eating nearly raw roast beef, drinking good Irish whiskey, and swimming twenty-two laps a day in an Olympic-sized swimming pool in forty-four minutes."

Someone groaned at the strenuousness of the exercise.

"The hardest part," Campbell added, "is keeping track of how many laps I've swum. So I hit on a method. I visualize in succession the twenty-two cards in the major arcana of the Tarot deck."

Some years later Joe and I nearly collided in one of the corridors at Chicago's O'Hare Airport. Glancing at our watches we decided that we had time for a sandwich before proceeding to our connecting flights, and during the lunch he recounted an incident I'll never forget.

Campbell told me that he was on his way from a lecture tour in the Bay Area, and he told his hosts not to meet him at the San Francisco Airport, for he had many friends in the area and would be renting a car. He just wanted to be told where his first appearance would be.

His hosts told him the event would be held in a synagogue in Marin, and to make sure he would be on time Campbell arrived a half hour early. Spotting the synagogue, he parked his car a decent distance from the entrance, got out, and started walking away, when a small boy about six years old said to him, "You can't park here."

Joe glanced around and said, "Why *can't* I park here? There's no NO PARKING sign, and no red stripe on the curb, so why can't I park here?"

The boy said, "Because I'm a fire hydrant."

Joe said he told the boy, "Oh, thank you! I could have gotten a parking ticket!"

With that he walked back to his car, unlocked it, and reparked it fifty feet away from the boy.

When we parted I found myself thinking that if there was anyone on the planet who could understand that a small boy could be a fire hydrant, that person would be Joseph Campbell.

THE YOUNG AVATAR

In 1968 the Krishnamurti Foundation flew me from MIT to interview Krishnamurti for an hour. They explained that they had hundreds of audiotapes of his lectures in Carnegie Hall and in Europe, but as yet they possessed no visual record of him.

It must be remembered that as a child Jiddu Krishnamurti had been adopted by the Theosophist Annie Besant and raised to be a world savior. But in his early twenties he renounced that role, saying that he would rather be a taxi driver than a world savior.

I was flown in the day before the interview so I could learn some background information about him from his secretary. The next day I did not lay eyes on him until we walked from opposite sides of the room onto the stage where the filming was to be done.

Over the years I have engaged in dozens of such interviews, but the one with Krishnamurti was unique. In the other interviews I thought I knew what the person I was interviewing thought. My job was to simply coax out his or her thoughts for the benefit of the audience. In this one, however, it was obvious before three minutes were up that I didn't have a clue where Krishnamurti's mind was. For the entire hour I was on my tiptoes reaching for what was beyond my grasp. That deflating realization that I did not know what he was going to say next continued until the cameras stopped rolling. Nevertheless, that sense of uncertainty makes this my favorite interview because it is more alive than the others.

I learned from that experience that Krishnamurti polarizes people. Some grasp his wisdom instantly; others never get it. I belong in the second camp, and Krishnamurti's secretary in the first. I asked this man what led him to emigrate from France to become Krishnamurti's secretary, a question that led to an intriguing story.

Paris is studded with small bookshops. In one of them the secretary was standing on a ladder perusing a top shelf. He pulled from it a book by an author he head never heard of, Jiddu Krishnamurti. The opening pages held him spellbound. The next thing he knew, two hours later, the proprietor was tugging at his trouser leg and telling him the bookstore was closing.

I am at the other extreme. I would not include Krishnamurti here were it not for the fact that two of the men I most respect, Aldous Huxley and David Bohm, looked up to him. And I must admit that every time I view the film of our interview I see a little more clearly the importance of what Krishnamurti was trying to say during that interview and during his career.

ANOTHER SHORT VIGNETTE

One morning, in the early 1960s, I answered my telephone, and Henry Wallace, the secretary of agriculture in the 1930s, and then vice president under Franklin Delano Roosevelt, was on the line. He said that he was in town for a lecture at Brandeis University that evening, and he asked if he could visit me that afternoon. His visit confirmed what I already knew, that he had deep personal interest in mysticism and Asian religions, for he spent an hour asking me about my encounter with Zen.

MY FRIENDSHIP WITH SAUL BELLOW

In the early 1980s, the novelist Saul Bellow spent three weeks at Syracuse University, where I was teaching in the philosophy department. His contract called for him to inaugurate his visit with a public lecture. Not surprisingly, so many people turned out for the lecture that even the largest auditorium could barely accommodate the crowd.

Kendra had an opportunity to thank him personally for his lecture, and she told him that *Henderson the Rain King* was her favorite of his books. It was so funny, she added, that she found herself laughing all the way through. In turn, he confessed to her that he wrote the book in an effort to pull himself out of a deep depression he was mired in at the time.

Later, Kendra told me that Saul's sense of "presence" to her, his deep attention while they were speaking, remains as vivid as her memory of his stunning lecture.

My turn came at the first of several colloquia his contract called for. Bellow had been asked to begin by putting forward an idea for discussion, which would be followed by two respondents, of which I was one. For his opening remarks, he chose to read a passage from Freud's *Moses and Monotheism*, followed by his acute observation: "Of course, historically it is nonsense, but what an interesting thing to have said!"

My response consisted of two questions. The first I thought was relevant but I was worried that the second might be considered impertinent.

"What was the most important book you have ever read?" I asked him. "And which book do you *wish* you had written?"

"Admiral Richard Byrd's *Alone* is the most important," he answered, "because no one else endured what he did and survived to tell the tale." And then he paused and added, "And the one I wish I had written is William J. Kennedy's *Ironweed*."

Then more tentatively I followed up with my second question.

"Now, Mr. Bellow, I hope that this next question isn't impertinent, but I must ask it. Time and time again in your books you describe a scene that rivets me to the page. And then, when you have my total attention, you slip in a paragraph that opens onto a transcendental world. So my question is this: Do you insert that for dramatic effect only, or do you think that that world really exists?"

Bellow offered a wry smile, and said, "Well, yes, the question is *indeed* impertinent." And then he proceeded to pretty much evade it. However, when the colloquium ended we found ourselves descending together in the elevator. He smiled wryly again and said, "I would like to see more of you while I am here."

Thus began a series of every-other-day lunches. He spent the mornings entering final changes in the page proofs of his next-to-last novel, *The Dean's December*, and then had lunch with me. During those hours we became friends, and he confided to me something that has since become common knowledge. When he was in Chicago he regularly attended a discussion group that met weekly to discuss the ideas of Rudolf Steiner, who, as is well-known, believed in transcendence.

Since being awarded the Nobel Prize for Literature, in 1976, Saul was a big fish, and Syracuse was a small puddle. When he arrived the local newspapers mounted a press conference in his honor. I chauffeured him to the event, which the convener opened by saying, "Mr. Bellow, you are a writer. We are all writers. What's the difference between us?"

Without batting an eye, Saul responded, "Reporters are interested in the news of the day. Novelists, if they are worth their salt, are interested in the news of eternity."

His quick wit, which he used not to elicit laughs but to drive points home, accounted for much of his success.

"One of the advantages of living in Chicago," he once said, "is that when a new idea reaches Chicago it is worn so thin that you have no trouble at all seeing through it."

If I had to choose one paragraph from his lifetime of writing, it would be this one from his short story "The Old System." I choose it for the sheer beauty of the writing, and for its hint of the transcendent:

> On the airport bus, he opened his father's copy of the Psalms. The black Hebrew letters only gaped at him like open mouths with tongues hanging down, pointing upward, flaming but dumb. He tried — forcing. It did no good. The tunnel, the swamps, the auto skeletons, machine entrails, dumps, gulls, sketchy Newark trembling in fiery summer, held his attention minutely.... Then in the plane running with concentrated fury to take off — the power to pull away from the magnetic earth, and more: When he saw the ground tilt backward, the machine rising from the runway, he said to himself in clear internal words, "Shema Yisroel," Hear, O Israel, God alone is God! On the right, New York leaned gigantically seaward, and the plane with a jolt of retracted wheels turned toward the river. The Hudson green within green, and rough with tide and wind. Isaac released the breath he had been holding, but sat belted tight. Above the marvelous bridges, over clouds, sailing in atmosphere, you know better than ever that you are no angel.

DAVID BOHM

Another of our illustrious visitors to Syracuse was the British quantum physicist David Bohm. The physics department eagerly anticipated his visit. The university faculty turned out in force for his opening lecture, which was also open to the general public.

"Everyone in the department cut their teeth on quantum mechanics by reading his book *Quantum Theory*," its chairman told me. "But he will not have a friendly audience."

Thus warned, I escorted Bohm to meet the physics department

in the largest auditorium on campus (the lecture had to be moved three times to accommodate the overflow audience), where Bohm was introduced.

He walked onstage and without referring to notes filled its two-tiered blackboard with equations. Within ten minutes he had lost everyone in the hall, except for the few specialists in his field.

Still, no one left.

When Bohm concluded his lecture, he sat down. One of those specialists stood up and said, "Professor Bohm, this is doubtless very interesting philosophy. But what has it got to do with physics?"

Startled, I glanced back at the blackboards. Not a word had been written on them; there were only numbers, equations, and formulas.

"I do not make that distinction," Bohm answered.

The physicists may have been alienated by the fact that Bohm was carrying on Einstein's infamous view that "God does not play dice with the universe." After all, Heisenberg's misnamed "indeterminacy principle" (*indeterminability* is the correct word) was in fashion then.

During Bohm's three-week stay at Syracuse, he and his wife, Sorel, Kendra, and I all became friends. When David died, Sorel wrote us an interesting account about him.

She said that David kept his office at London University and would spend his days working in it. On agreement, he would phone his wife, and when he was leaving his office, he would hail a cab to take him to the Tube; upon emerging from the Underground, he would catch another cab to their apartment.

On the day that Bohm died, on October 27, 1992, he happened to add to his customary message, "It's been an exciting day. I think I'm on to something."

To this day, I wonder if that was prescient.

A MONK'S LIFE

I have been invited to so many conferences and have had to submit my regrets so often that it was a pleasure to receive a follow-up invitation, in 1968, to an ecumenical conference in Calcutta, India, that listed Thomas Merton as one of the scheduled speakers.

Seeing his name on the list compelled me to change my mind, for he had worked his way to the top of the list of persons I most wanted to meet.

The conference was slated to open with a 5:00 p.m. reception on the lawn behind the hotel that housed us. I was prompt, but Merton was already present, sitting at a table and sipping a soft drink. I joined him and wasted no time engaging him in conversation. He was the true celebrity at the conference, and I wasn't certain whether I would catch him alone again.

I began very honestly, confessing to him, "I could never have been a monk. My attraction to women is too strong in me. But I do have a contemplative streak in me. So I've often wondered what a monk's life is like. So, Thomas, what *is* a monk's life like?"

Of all the answers in the world, his was the last one I expected.

"Well, it's very nice," he said, simply.

"Your answer surprises me," I told him. "I would find the three vows difficult."

"Oh, those!" he said, laughing. "Poverty is a snap. Chastity is more difficult, but manageable. But obedience — obedience is a bugger!"

As it turned out, I was able to have quite a bit of time with Merton, and we became fast friends.

Merton was scheduled to be the last speaker. There were many television crews converging on the conference, and he was asked to wear his clerical collar. He began his address by saying that he felt as if he was appearing in disguise, in costume. In his usual garb of dungarees and work shirt, he usually felt more like a hermit.

But he became more serious when he talked about representing the people who didn't count so much in the eyes of the general public: monks, the poor, and poets. Then he added:

> So I stand among you as one who offers a small message of hope, that first, there are always people who dare to seek on the margin of society, who are not dependent on social acceptance, not dependent on social routine, and prefer a kind of free-floating existence under a state of risk. And among these people, if they are faithful to their own calling, to their own vocation, and to their own message from God, communication on the deepest level is possible. And the deepest level of communication is not communication, but communion. It is wordless. It is beyond words, and it is beyond speech, and it is beyond concept. Not that we discover a new unity. We discover an older unity...we are already one. But we imagine that we are not. And what we have to recover is our original unity. What we have to be is what we are.

Following the conference, Merton and I were scheduled to fly to New Delhi to catch connecting flights, and we agreed to sit together on the plane. During the flight I mentioned that I had always wanted to take the pilgrimage from Kathmandu to Pokhara, a major monastery in one of the world's most majestic settings.

"The plane trip took only fifteen minutes," I told him, "and the journey on foot, which undulates up and down the mountainsides, takes seventeen days. But it's a real pilgrimage."

Tom picked up on my remark, and we became slaphappy.

"Let's do it," he said. "I will wire my superior back in Kentucky and tell him he can defrock me if he has to. You wire Kendra and tell her she can divorce you if she must. But we are pilgrimaging from Kathmandu to Pokhara!"

The pilot's announcement that our plane was landing jolted us out of our pilgrimage fantasies, and once in the airport we parted ways, I to head to the north to visit the Tibetans, and Tom to fly south to Burma and to his death. Tragically, he died later that evening in his hotel room due to a live electrical wire that was lying on the wet floor as he was taking a shower.

He was only fifty-three.

DINNER WITH THE ROCKEFELLERS

One afternoon, in the early 1970s, a friend called from San Francisco and asked if Kendra and I would like to come to her house for dinner. She apologized for the suddenness of the invitation and explained that she was hosting Laurance Rockefeller, who had told her that he would like to meet me.

How could I resist such an invitation?

Over dinner, he explained that he had just returned from Japan, where he had gone to try to determine why their automobile industry was surpassing ours.

"Can you shine some light on the situation?" he asked me.

"Well, I'm not sure," I said. "But it might have to do with the fact that Japanese workers work six days a week and take only two weeks off for vacation. I recently read that last year they took only 5.2 of their allotted 6 days of annual vacation. Maybe when auto workers in Detroit show that kind of loyalty we might find ourselves catching up with the Japanese."

Of course, that was three decades ago and conditions in the world's auto industry have changed dramatically, but at the time the comments seemed germane.

"Have you noticed, Laurance, that taxi drivers in Japan dress in white shirts, black pants, and polished shoes, and before they go on shift they lift their voices in song as they dedicate the day to serving their nation, their company, and their passengers?"

Looking back on this exchange I think what I was trying to

convey to Laurance was my admiration for loyalty, community, even a certain esprit de corps that I have always found in Japanese culture.

THE GIFT

For several years, the Lithuanian-Polish poet Czeslaw Milosz and his wife were neighbors of ours when we lived in the Berkeley Hills. We became good friends, and we would frequently have supper together. One evening, as he and I were nursing our drinks in our kitchen I told him a story that elicited from him the heartiest belly laugh I have ever heard. Knowing that there was no more love lost between the Lithuanians and the Germans than there was between the Austrians and the Germans, I passed on to him a joke that I had recently heard.

A German storm trooper came upon a group of Austrians who seemed to be malingering on the job. "Why aren't you working?" he demanded. "We *are* working," they insisted. "We were told to dismantle that wall, and we are trying to figure out how to do it." Commenting that the wall didn't look very sturdy to him, the German went over to it and gave it a slight shove. It promptly toppled over. "Well, all right, if you are going to use force..."

I thought the walls of our kitchen were going to buckle outward from Czeslaw's thundering laughter.

Some time later, Czeslaw received an award for being an outstanding Lithuanian poet. We toasted him for receiving that honor, which meant more to him than the innumerable others that had been bestowed on him, because Lithuanian was his native language.

When the Miloszes returned from Lithuania, we invited them back to dinner and asked them how the occasion turned out.

"It was a disaster," Czeslaw said, sadly. "I was so elated about the award that I had four double vodka martinis on the flight over, and they knocked me down. I couldn't get out of bed the next day to receive the award at the state dinner."

The Miloszes have since died, but they are not forgotten. A poem of Czeslaw's hangs framed on Kendra's study wall.

GIFT

A day so happy.
Fog lifted early, I worked in the garden.
Hummingbirds were stopping over honeysuckle flowers.
There was no thing on earth I wanted to possess.
I knew no one worth my envying him.
Whatever evil I had suffered, I forgot.
To think that once I was the same man did not embarrass me.
In my body I felt no pain.
When straightening up, I saw the blue sea and sails.

To some extent, our friendship with the Miloszes has been replaced by our friendship with Charles Towns and his wife. Charles received the Nobel Prize in Physics for discovering the laser. Soon after, publishers leaned heavily on him to write his autobiography. At first, Charles wasn't interested. Eventually, however, he agreed to write an account, on the condition that the book be titled not *How I Discovered the Laser*, but instead, *How the Laser Happened*.

When the book appeared, Kendra and I went to the kickoff event at our neighborhood bookstore. Charles opened the event by describing a cartoon in which a beaver is speaking to a muskrat as they look up at the towering Boulder Dam.

"No," says the beaver. "I didn't exactly build it. They just picked up on one of my ideas."

In his own humble way, Towns was making the point that *he* didn't invent the laser. There were thirty or forty loose pieces of the puzzle lying around on the table, as it were, and he just happened to come up with the missing piece.

AN ENCOUNTER WITH WILLIAM HEWLETT

I was slow on the uptake with William Hewlett. Two or three decades ago I received a letter from him that said he and a group of friends had been reading and discussing my book on the world's religions. They wanted to meet and discuss the book with its author. If he sent me a round-trip ticket to their local airport, somewhere in western Texas, would I be willing to fly down and spend a morning discussing the subject with them?

Always interested in the subject of religion — arguably the most vitally important subject there is — I accepted the invitation.

Hewlett met me at the airport, and when we were in his car and on our way to his house, I said that he obviously knew more about me that I knew about him.

"Would you please balance the equation," I asked him, "by telling me something about yourself?"

Hewlett told me that he and his partner, Bill Packard, had invented a gadget, an audio oscillator that had helped launch one of the first electronics companies in the world. When the company was set solidly in place, he turned its management over to his business partner and cofounder, David Packard. His primary interest now, Hewitt added, was in the Monday-morning gatherings that focused on what was uppermost in the participants' minds.

Hewlett's house, it turned out, was a veritable mansion. It boasted a huge living room, where about fifty people sat, awaiting our arrival. Their questions were pertinent, and the discussions they provoked were lively. But it would be pointless to summarize them here. What is important is the way that day ended.

Later that night, when I was back home, I sat down at my desk for a moment before starting to bed. My eyes happened to fall on the engine that powers my computer and printer. That was when I noticed, to my astonishment, that embossed on it were the letters "HP." I had just spent the day with Hewlett, of Hewlett-Packard fame.

THE WISDOM OF FAITH

During the filming of the PBS series I did with Bill Moyers, its director wanted a location shot with the two of us and asked if we would walk together for half a block down a street in Manhattan, outside the studio. She asked us to look natural and try to have a casual conversation. I used the occasion to ask Bill a burning question rather than just stage an exchange between us.

"You were Lyndon Johnson's press secretary for two years," I said, as if I needed to remind him. "What was your take on him?"

Bill smiled and said, "He was twelve of the most complicated men I have ever met."

Tantalizingly, he added that he hoped to write a book about the president when he retired.

It goes without saying that the Moyers series *The Wisdom of Faith* boosted my public career more than anything else that ever happened to me. But what means even more to me is that he befriended me before I even recognized his name.

To wit. One day the phone rang, and Bill announced himself on the other end of the line. He told me that he was coming to the Bay Area and would like to meet me. I told him that regrettably I was going to be away during the time he was here. He responded that he could fly me to New York.

Soon after I was on a plane to New York and grabbed a taxi at the airport to take me to his hotel in Manhattan. I went to his suite and discovered to my surprise that he had set up an array of cameras to film our conversation.

When Bill saw me enter, he strode across the room and greeted me with a warm smile, extended his hand, and said, "Huston, we have known each other for a long time."

To my delight, it turned out that he had read *The Religions of Man*, the title of the first edition of *The World's Religions*. As a former student of theology, he had found something in the book that had moved him and he vowed that someday he would meet me and interview me for one of his notable documentaries.

Our evening was very enjoyable. As the viewing public now knows, Bill has a talent for putting people at ease on camera. And yet what really surprised me was the touching letter he sent to me when I returned to Berkeley. I treasure it to this day. The letter also provides a note of rejoicing and a coda to this chapter.

Dear Huston,

I couldn't have been more excited about the evening together. You were engaging, witty, wise, and eloquent, and I am stirred to want to do another round with you to see if I can then raise the funds to turn the whole of the material into a three-part miniseries on PBS. We didn't even cover your time in China or Confucianism or a lot of what I wanted to treat from the other religions you have mastered. So I will be in touch later to see if there is a day we can meet in your part of the country — perhaps in that Japanese garden you mentioned — and continue.

By the way, we finished at the right time. Soon after you and I left the room the chandelier above our heads came loose and crashed to the floor. The gods must have been angry. Warm regards — and much appreciation,

Bill

Chapter Seventeen

How Philosophy Heals

A t first glance, the title of this chapter may sound strange, for although I have a doctorate in philosophy, it would be fraudulent to follow my name with "MD." But that is because, in the course of time, the definition of the word *healing* has narrowed to the point that it is now considered to be only the province of physicians and therapists.

It used to be otherwise, as the following samples clearly indicate: *The Concise Modern Oxford English Dictionary* defines *therapy* as "a treatment intended to relieve or cure a disorder." It does not seem too self-serving to point out that that definition does not stipulate that the disorder must be physical; in fact, it could refer to a logical disorder in an argument.

Therapeia is the title of Robert Earl Cushman's book, which he subtitles *Plato's Conception of Philosophy*. Neal Grossman titles

his book on Spinoza *Healing the Mind*. In a monograph on the Py-
thagoreans, Aristotle mentions Pythagoras's interest in medicinal
plants, including the "sacred" qualities of the mallow plant. The
passage concludes by noting that as Pythagoras went around from
town to town, word went out that Pythagoras was coming, not to
teach but to heal.

The early Greeks called their philosophers *soters*, or saviors.
Thus the word *philosophy* comes from *philo* (the love of) and *So-
phia* (divine wisdom), which, significantly, is feminine. Alterna-
tively, philosophy is the love of divine wisdom, especially as it
deals with ultimate matters.

Etched in stone above the entrance of the third-century BCE
Library of Alexandria, built by Ptolemy (and, rumor has it, ac-
cidentally burned down by Julius Caesar), was a marvelous motto:
"The Place for the Healing of the Soul."

The above items document the fact that originally *healing*
referred to more things than just physical healing, including philosophy, but it leaves unaddressed the question of *how?* How does
philosophy heal in this wider sense?

Diagnosis precedes prescription.

Physicians do not prescribe medicines until they have aligned
the medicine with the malady that the medicine is designed to cure.
So I begin with the ailment, the disease for which philosophy is the
cure. This will require a long paragraph, for I want to be a careful
diagnostician.

There lies within even the blithest, most lighthearted among
us a fundamental *dis-ease*. It acts like an unquenchable thirst that
renders many of us incapable of ever coming to full peace.

This desire lies in the marrow of our bones and the deep re-
cesses of our souls. All great literature, poetry, art, philosophies,
psychologies, and religions try to name and analyze this longing.

We are seldom in direct touch with it, and indeed the modern world seems set on preventing us from getting in touch with it by covering it over with an unending phantasmagoria of entertainments, obsessions, addictions, and distractions of every sort.

Still, the longing is there, built into us like a jack-in-the-box that presses for release. Two great paintings suggest this longing in their titles: Paul Gauguin's *Where Did We Come From? What Are We? Where Are We Going?* and Giorgio de Chirico's *The Nostalgia of the Infinite*. But I must work with words. Whether or not we realize it, simply to be human is to long for release from mundane existence with its confining walls of finitude and mortality.

At the risk of belaboring this point, I will spell it out. Blindness is an affliction. And as we all want to move from where we are not comfortable to an easy chair, so to speak, we want the scales to be removed from our eyes so we can see again, and philosophy is the way we learn how to see the world more clearly.

The argument is conclusive: philosophy is a healing art. Here are two final examples to prove the point.

THE TWO CATEGORICAL, UNCONDITIONAL VIRTUES

There are two and only two virtues that are categorical in the sense that they do not have to be qualified to be true: they are gratitude and empathy, the latter being the capacity to work one's way into the feelings of others and to feel them as if they were one's own.

Love is the runner-up, but it doesn't quite make it. I will use St. Paul as a foil to show why it doesn't. For a comprehensive and poetic description of love, I can think of nothing that surpasses St. Paul's poetic panegyric in First Corinthians, which sets its tone in its opening verse, which reads as follows:

> Though I speak with tongues of men and of angels and have not
>   love,
> I am but clanging brass and tinkling cymbal.

and it climaxes by concluding that:

> Now abideth faith, hope and love, these three,
> and the greatest of these is love.

That is very well put, and I cite it here because it takes Paul thirteen verses of scripture to pinpoint the *kind* of love he is talking about, with "smotherlove" being a glaring example of a love that he does not want to include. Jesus's summons to *"Do unto others as you would do that they should do unto you"* is a striking call to *enact* sympathy.

What can activate the will is the too-often-overlooked sentiment of empathy. It can resound like a mantra in our deep, subliminal minds and keep our lives on course. And it is evinced in the widening gap between the rich and the poor that is making a growing number of economists wonder if capitalism is a viable economic system. This worry elicits from me a few lines that turned out to look something like a poem. It reads like this:

> Pity not those who lack for roof and bread —
> Dumb, blocked years ahead — pity not those,
> But let compassion reign
> For the one percent that rake in seventy percent
> Of our wealth
> And feel no shame for justice dead.

I find it interesting to speculate what the world would be like if empathy were the warp and woof of human relationships. It seems possible to me that we would then be close — or at least closer — to realizing the Kingdom of God on Earth.

Epilogue

Famous Last Words

Innumerable last words have been recorded, but the words of two people especially have etched themselves into my memory so much that they are always with me.

The first words were uttered by an eighteenth-century writer, Lady Mary Wortley Montagu, who said before she died, "It's all been very interesting."

Well, it certainly has been. I have to suppress the impulse to resort to the vernacular and say, "You can certainly say that again!" Instead I will extend the Lady Montagu's assertion with a quatrain from *Markings* by the second secretary-general of the United Nations, Dag Hammarskjöld:

How long the road is. But, for all the time the journey has already taken, how you have needed every second of it in order to learn what the road passes by.

The other last words that I shall report were uttered by an early church father and archbishop of Constantinople who died in 407. His given name was John, but Chrysostom, meaning "golden mouth," was later added on because of his remarkable oratorical powers.

He was ascetically inclined, and he angered both ecclesiastic and political authorities, including Aelia Eudoxia, the wife of the Byzantine emperor Arcadius, for denouncing the abuse of authority. For this rebuke, he was banished several times, and it was during the last of these banishments, which included a forced march that taxed his aged body beyond endurance, that he collapsed and died.

There is no extant record of his last words, but there is a strong oral tradition that those words were, "Thanks, thanks for everything. Praise, praise for it all."

If circumstances permit, I would like those to be my last words as well.

Notes

PROLOGUE. OH, HAPPY DAY

xxvi *When we are persuaded that it is the hand of God*: *Brother Lawrence: His Conversations and Letters on the Practice of the Presence of God* (London: J. Hatchard and Son, 1824).

CHAPTER SEVEN.
A GLOBE-CIRCLING ADVENTURE

73 *The Mela is an 85-day-long assembly*: The Kumbh Mela is the world's largest mass pilgrimage. Millions of Hindus gather every twelve years at Allabad, Haridwar, Uijain, and Nashik to bathe in the Ganges for ritual purification.

74 *Wonderful is sound*: *Guru Granth Sahib* (New Delhi: Ravi Sachdev, 1960).

CHAPTER NINE.
MAGIC AND MYSTERY
ON THE ROOF OF THE WORLD

99   *When I count my teachers of science*: His Holiness the Dalai
Lama, *The Universe in a Single Atom: The Convergence of
Science and Spirituality* (New York: Morgan Road/Double-
day, 2005), 99.

101 *On the bulletin board in the front hall*: Richard Selzer, *Mortal
Lessons: Notes on the Art of Surgery* (1974; repr., New York:
Harcourt, 1996), 33–36.

CHAPTER TWELVE. IMPROBABLES

124 *Calm eyes a-look 'cross sea*: Patience Worth, *The Sorry Tale:
A Story of the Time of Christ* (New York: Henry Holt & Co.,
1917), vii.

CHAPTER THIRTEEN.
PRIMAL RELIGIONS, PRIMAL PASSIONS

138 *Greeting and thanks to each other as people*: The Thanksgiving Address is a traditional prayer of the Seneca Nation.

CHAPTER FIFTEEN. WHAT'S IT ALL ABOUT?

151 *Peter, it's not too much to cite you*: Huston Smith, "Scientism:
The Bedrock of the Modern World View," www.world
wisdom.com/public/library/default.aspx.

CHAPTER SIXTEEN. FAME AT MY ELBOW

158 *Today almost no one has heard of Gerald Heard*: Adapted
from the introduction of Gerald Heard, *Pain, Sex, and
Time: A New Outlook on Evolution and the Future of Man*
(1939; repr., Rhinebeck, NY: Monkfish, 2004).

161 *There was a moment in the 1950s*: Huston Smith, "Remembering Aldous Huxley," *Los Angeles Times*, November 20, 1988.

164 *God is*: Aldous Huxley, "Being," *Huxley and God: Essays on Religious Experience*, ed. Jacqueline Hazard Bridgeman (New York: Crossroad, 2003), 15–16.

179 *On the airport bus*: Saul Bellow, "The Old System," *Saul Bellow: Collected Stories*, ed. Janis Bellow (New York: Penguin, 2001), 114.

182 *So I stand among you*: From an informal talk delivered in Calcutta, October 1968, in Thomas Merton, *Echoing Silence: Thomas Merton on the Vocation of Writing*, ed. Robert Inchausti (Boston: New Seed/Shambhala, 2007), 78.

185 *A day so happy*: Czeslaw Milosz, "Gift," *Czeslaw Milosz: Selected Poems, 1931–2004* (New York: HarperCollins, 2006), 104.

EPILOGUE. FAMOUS LAST WORDS

194 *How long the road is*: Dag Hammarskjöld, *Markings*, trans. Leif Sjöberg and W. H. Auden (1964; repr., New York: Ballantine, 1983), 68.

Index

E

Egypt, 65–67
Einstein, Albert, 166
Eliot, T. S., 149, 167
empathy, 191–92
energy, human, 173
England, 58–60
enlightenment experience, 45–55
entheogens, 28
ESP, 163
Europe, 61–65
    See also specific country
evangelical meetings, 22–25
evolution, 159
existence, 143–48

F

Fayette, Missouri, 25–29
feng shui, 16
festivals and celebrations, 73–74,
    75–77, 83–84
First Great Awakening, 22
Forster, E. M., 153
France, 61–62
Freud, Sigmund, 151–53, 177
fringe phenomena, 173
full-lotus position, 45–48

G

Galbraith, John Kenneth, 172–73
Garauon, Raymond, 87
Garrett, Eileen, 126
Gilbert, Kenneth, 87
God, 165

Golden Temple, 74–75
Goto Zuigan Roshi, 47–55
Grateful Dead, 104–6
gratitude, 54–55, 191–92
Graves, Robert, 170–71
Great Chain of Being, The (Love-
    joy), 150
Great Going Forth, 17–20
Greece, 63, 78–79
Greene, Elmer, 173
Greeting of Thanks to the Natural
    World, 138–39
Grossman, Neal, 189–90
guardian angels, 10–12, 14–15
Gustavus Adolphus College, 18
Gyuto monks, 105–6

H

Hahn, Thich Nhat, 85
Haiti, 114–15
Hall, Tom, 35–36
Hammarskjöld, Dag, 193–94
harp, 129–30
Hart, Mickey, 104–6
Harvard Divinity School, 100
hatha yoga, 71–72
healing, 101–4, 189–92
Healing the Mind (Grossman), 190
Heard, Gerald, 157–60, 169
Heisenberg, Werner, 169–70, 180
Henderson the Rain King (Bellow),
    177
Henry, Gray, 66–67
Hewlett, William, 186–87
Himalayan Mountains, 93–106
Hindus, 75, 77

M

Mahabharata, 83
majlis, 75–77
Manual of Zen Buddhism (Suzuki),
   45
Masai warriors, 107–12
Mazatlán, Mexico, 139–41
McClure, George, 35
medicine, Tibetan, 101–4
meditation, 68, 77–78, 125, 160,
   164–66
mediumship, 124
mental evolution, 159
meritocracy, 5–6
Merton, Thomas, 181–83
metaphysics, 150
Methodists, 22, 128
Mexico, 36–37, 127–28
Milosz, Czeslaw, 184–85
Missouri, 21–25
MIT (Massachusetts Institute
   of Technology), 96–97, 99,
   161–62, 170
monks, Tibetan, 105–6
Montagu, Mary Wortley, 193
Moral Man and Immoral Society
   (Niebuhr), 172
Morris, R. B., xxix–xxx
Mortal Lessons (Selzer), 101–4
mortification, 165
Moses and Monotheism (Freud),
   177
Mount Athos (Greece), 78–79
Moyers, Bill, 187–88
Muhammad, 76

multiphonic chanting, 95–97,
   105–6
Muslims, 74–75
Myanmar, 67–68
Myoshinji, 47, 50–55
mysticism, 157, 162
myth, 173

N

Native American Church,
   139–42
Native American Freedom
   Restoration Act, 141
Native American Rights Fund
   (NARF), 134–35
Native Americans, 131–42
Neihardt, John, 122–23
Nepal, 77–78
never agains, 6–8
Newman, Cardinal, 36
Niebuhr, Reinhold, 172
Nothingness, 161

O

Oakland Symphony Orchestra,
   129
Olduvai Gorge (South Africa),
   107, 110, 111–12
One Nation under God (Snake),
   142
Onondaga seminar, 137–39
Oppenheimer, Robert, 150, 166
Origins of Love and Hate (Suttie),
   152–53

About Huston Smith

H uston Smith is recognized and revered as the preeminent teacher of world religions. Smith has taught at Washington University, the Massachusetts Institute of Technology, Syracuse University, and the University of California, Berkeley. He has written fifteen books, including the classic *The World's Religions*, which has sold over two million copies in many translations, and the *New York Times* bestseller *Why Religion Matters*. He has been bestowed with twelve honorary degrees and was the focus of the five-part television series *The Wisdom of Faith* hosted by Bill Moyers.

About Phil Cousineau

P hil Cousineau is a freelance writer, editor, photographer, filmmaker, creativity consultant, and literary tour leader. He has published over twenty-five books, including the worldwide bestseller *The Art of Pilgrimage*, for which Huston Smith wrote the foreword. Cousineau has written or cowritten eighteen documentary films and contributed to forty-two other books. Currently, he is the host and cowriter of the nationally broadcast television series *Global Spirit* on PBS. His forthcoming books are *The Painted Word* and *Who Stole the Arms of the Venus de Milo?*